ECSTASY WITHIN DISCIPLINE
The Poetry of Richard Wilbur

American Academy of Religion
Academy Series

edited by
Susan Thistlethwaite

Number 85
ECSTASY WITHIN DISCIPLINE
The Poetry of Richard Wilbur
by
John B. Hougen

John B. Hougen

ECSTASY WITHIN DISCIPLINE
The Poetry of Richard Wilbur

Scholars Press
Atlanta, Georgia

ECSTASY WITHIN DISCIPLINE
The Poetry of Richard Wilbur

by
John B. Hougen

© 1995
The American Academy of Religion

ECSTASY WITHIN DISCIPLINE
The Poetry of Richard Wilbur

by
John B. Hougan

Library of Congress Cataloging in Publication Data
Hougen, John B.
   Ecstasy within discipline : the poetry of Richard Wilbur / John B.
Hougan.
      p. cm. — (American Academy of Religion academy series ; no.
85)
   Includes bibliographical references.
   ISBN 1-55540-959-8 (alk. paper). — ISBN 1-55540-960-1 (pbk. :
alk. paper)
   1. Wilbur, Richard, 1921-   —Criticism and interpretation.
I. Title. II. Series.
PS3545.I32165Z68 1995
811'.52—dc20   94-783
                                           CIP

Printed in the United States of America
on acid-free paper

To Marcia . . . who waited

TABLE OF CONTENTS

ACKNOWLEDGEMENTS

Nathan A Scott, Jr., of the University of Virginia, served as director of this project in its first incarnation. His own affection for Richard Wilbur's poetry, his stubborn refusal to accept anything less than my best work, his personal support, and especially his capacious breadth of vision all gave shape and substance to my dissertation. As time passes, I keep discovering that I owe him more.

J. C. Levenson (also of the University of Virginia), with his love of fine poetry, provided the ideal classroom context in which to discover Richard Wilbur. Then, throughout the writing of this study, he was always available to talk over my thoughts, point out connections between Wilbur and other poets, affirm the importance of Wilbur's art and insights for our troubled times, and provide warm encouragement. I am most grateful.

Others at UVA without whom I cannot imagine having brought this work to completion include Larry Bouchard, Dan Via, Bill King, Clark Brittain, Clinton Kersey, John Sykes, Perry Kea, Tom Reardon, and Jerome Colegrove, as well as the staff and congregation of St. Mark Lutheran Church, Charlottesville (and later, PALM Campus Ministry, Columbia, S.C.), who were able to see some advantage in having one of their pastors assume the dual roles of scholar and priest.

Finally, I acknowledge a whole network of family and friends which sustains and supports, the far-flung community to which I belong. From among them I single out for special thanks Carol Krebs, Andrew Hertler, and Randy Bishop who provided the necessary patience, good humor, and technical competence to bring this manuscript into final form.

John B. Hougen
August 1995

Teresa

After the sun's eclipse,
The brighter angel and the spear which drew
A bridal outcry from her open lips,
    She could not prove it true,
Nor think at first of any means to test
By what she had been wedded or possessed.

    Not all cries were the same;
There was an island in mythology
Called by the very vowels of her name
    Where vagrants of the sea,
Changed by a wand, were made to squeal and cry
As heavy captives in a witch's sty.

    The proof came soon and plain:
Visions were true which quickened her to run
God's barefoot errands in the rocks of Spain
    Beneath its beating sun,
And lock the O of ecstasy within
The tempered consonants of discipline.

                Richard Wilbur

The imagination . . . when in best health neither slights the world of fact
nor stops with it, but seeks the invisible through the visible.

                Richard Wilbur

INTRODUCTION

This study of Richard Wilbur's poetry stresses the importance of Wilbur's religious sensibilities for understanding, on the one hand, the formal focus of his work, and, on the other, Wilbur's place in twentieth century American poetry. Throughout his career Wilbur has defied the conventional wisdom which holds that the formal resources of poetry are instruments of control to be used by poets in their attempts to make manageable either inner turmoil or the world's chaos. Wilbur's verse almost always employs regular metrical patterns, rhyme and other sonic devices, but for the purpose of recounting experiences of transcendence. Therefore, his poetry is not a means to rationalize the irrational, but an effort to increase our awareness of a mystery.

Chapter One places Wilbur's work in the context of American poetry and criticism at mid-century. I claim that his work has more in common with the innovative poetics of that era than is usually recognized. Similarities among the works of Wilbur and his peers become more obvious when they are viewed as part of larger literary movements: here, twentieth century American verse and Romanticism. Chapter Two summarizes the epistemological assumptions that give shape to Wilbur's poems. He writes as one committed to objectivity but also keenly aware that the perceiver's constructive imagination influences both what is perceived and how perceptions become integrated into life and thought. Chapters Three and Four delineate several strategies by which Wilbur regularly carries his readers along "seeking the invisible through the visible" (Wilbur). These strategies include, but are not limited to, those noticed by Louis Martz in English metaphysical poetry and which led him to posit a genre he called "meditative poetry." The fifth and final chapter presents Wilbur's vision of the relationship between transcendence and the world of fact. His spirituality is compared and contrasted with that of Emerson, Frost, Christian Scripture, Thomas Merton, and Emily Dickinson. Wilbur's vision draws heavily on Christian resources as it asserts over and over again that in ecstasy what has been separated may be reconciled, and that ecstasy is possible through spiritual and literary discipline.

Chapter One

FORMAL POETRY: WILBUR IN CONTEXT

Let me try to list some of the virtues that distinguish the poetry of Richard Wilbur. First of all, a superb ear (unequaled, I think, in the work of any poet now writing in English) for stately measure, cadences of a slow, processional grandeur, and a rich, ceremonial orchestration. A philosophic bent and a religious temper, which are by no means the same thing, but which here consort comfortably together. Wit, polish, a formal elegance that is never haughty or condescending, though certain freewheeling poets take it for a chilling frigidity. And an unfeigned gusto, a naturally happy and grateful response to the physical beauty of life, of women, of works of art, landscapes, weather, and the perceiving, constructing mind that tries to know them. But in a way I think most characteristic of all, his is the most kinetic poetry I know: verbs are among his conspicuously important tools, and his poetry is everywhere a vision of action, of motion and performance.

Anthony Hecht

Anthony Hecht's celebration of Richard Wilbur's sensibilities and craftsmanship is typical of the response Wilbur has elicited from the literary community for nearly forty-five years. His prominence in American letters is firmly grounded in the esteem of his peers. Nearly all agree that he is a "peerless craftsman" and "one of the few living American masters of formal verse."[1] One finds his genius for prosody and his commitment to strict metrical patterns all the more remarkable since he matured as a poet when

---

[1]Wendy Salinger, "Introduction," in *Richard Wilbur's Creation*, ed. Wendy Salinger (Ann Arbor: The University of Michigan Press, 1983), 1. Brad Leithauser, "Richard Wilbur at Sixty," in Salinger, 282.

the prevailing assumption in American poetry was that metrics and sonics, rhyme and wit, more often inhibited vitality than they released it.

It is no doubt Wilbur's reliance on traditional poetic forms in an era when they were out of fashion that muted the praise of his work in some quarters and in others gave rise to blatantly negative criticism. Randall Jarrell's and Peter Viereck's reservations about Wilbur's early poems were cited by later reviewers and have set the tone for many negative estimates of his work.[2] Jarrell, Viereck, and their followers seemed to say that, because of their formality, Wilbur's poems were dull, bland, removed from real life in the world, and indicated an inordinate need to control internal and external chaos. As Jarrell once remarked,

> Somebody said about Christopher Fry . . . "I don't think real poetry is ever as poetic as this." One feels this way about some of Mr. Wilbur's language. . . . [The reader] is sure to start longing for a murder or a character-after thirty or forty pages of *Ceremony* he would pay dollars for one dramatic monologue, some blessed graceless human voice that has not yet learned to express itself so composedly as poets do. . . . Mr. Wilbur never goes too far, but he never goes far enough. . . . I can't blame his readers if they say to him in encouraging impatient voices: "Come on, take a chance!"[3]

Peter Viereck, with more concision, stated that Wilbur "has all the qualities of a great artist except vulgarity."[4] Implicit in the comments of Jarrell and Viereck is the notion that formality is untrue to the richness, complexity, vulgarity, and violence of the world, that it is unsuitable for poetry which deals mimetically with war, lovers, death, nature and the quest for order and understanding in the midst of life's mysteries and contingencies. Later critics

---

[2]At times both Jarrell and Viereck were also lavish in their praise of Wilbur's emerging talent. See: Randall Jarrell, "From 'Fifty Years of American Poetry,'" in Salinger, 85; Randall Jarrell, "From 'A View of Three Poets,'" in Salinger, 46-47; and Peter Viereck, "From 'Technique and Inspiration-A Year of Poetry,'" in Salinger, 50.

[3]Randall Jarrell, *Poetry and the Age* (New York: Vintage Books, 1953), 227-230.

[4]Viereck, in Salinger, 50.

voiced this complaint either mildly (as with Thom Gunn: "His earlier work . . was at times too smart and facile"), or harshly, as with Theodore Holmes:[5]

> [Wilbur] takes refuge . . . in the despair of style. Holding up the things of this world in their own ultimate status in ontology as a solution to the dilemmas of human existence can only be satisfactory for the privileged and unthinking, for to the others of us who must bear their weight they contain within them the very problems which these poems take them as solving. It is the purview of things seen from the Parnassian heights of wealth, privilege, ease, refinement, and education, looking down on the permanent sufferings of humanity without being part of them. The poems seem almost at times a dance [of] . . . rhyme, meter, myth, history, reference, obscurity, and precious intellection, that would reconcile us to our trouble without comprehending it.

Edward Pygge parodied Wilbur's style, calling his poem "Occam's Razor Starts in Massachusetts." Its final lines express a view of Wilbur's work similar to that of Viereck and Holmes:

> . . . this lyric
> Where learning deftly intromits precision:
> The shots are Parthian, the victories Pyrrhic.
> Banquo's ghost was not so pale a vision.
>
> But still you must concede this boy's got class.
> His riddles lead through vacuums to a space
> Where skill leans on the parapet of farce
> And sees Narcissus making up his face.[6]

It is my opinion that the greater part of the negative critical response which greeted Wilbur's work, and which persists in some quarters even today, stems from partisanship in the disputes that arose among American

---

[5]Thom Gunn, "From 'Imitations and Originals,'" in Salinger, 70. Theodore Holmes, "Wilbur's New Book-Two Views: I. A Prophet Without a Prophecy," in Salinger, 73.

[6]Edward Pygge, "Occam's Razor Starts in Massachusetts," in *The Brand-X Anthology of Poetry*, ed. William Zaranka (Cambridge: Apple-wood Books, Inc., 1981), 306-7.

poets and literary theorists at mid-century. By that time, Cleanth Brooks and
Robert Penn Warren had seen their textbook *Understanding Poetry* (1938)
transformed from what they intended (a guidebook to help students
experience poems) into the vade mecum of the New Criticism. Many of the
poems written in the forties and fifties, therefore, contained all the elements
Brooks and Warren had identified as constituents of poetic expression. But,
however correctly they were written, many were inferior works, for they
contained none of the life of great poetry. So a counter-revolution was
bound to be launched, and, indeed, after a time such poets as Ginsberg and
Berryman and Olson began to try to breathe new life into American literature.
They and others wanted poetry that was new, and a poet like Wilbur
appeared to be a part of an old guard that had to be displaced.[7] For he, far
from repudiating the generation of poets that had preceded him, publicly
defended the poetics implied by *Understanding Poetry.*[8] And, in both verse
and prose, Wilbur set himself apart from the modishness he perceived in the
poetic innovations that began in the fifties.

"Flippancies" (*MR:NCP* 90),[9] first published in 1975, is a playful poke
at some of his peers. Wilbur returns their criticism of him by suggesting that
the non-conforming poetic movements of the fifties have taken on the very

---

[7]Clive James, "When The Gloves Are Off," in Salinger, 107.

[8]Richard Wilbur, "The Genie in the Bottle," in *Mid-Century American Poets*, ed.
John Ciardi (New York: Twayne Publishers, Inc., 1950), 7. Wilbur, "On My Own Work,"
in *Responses: Prose Pieces*: 1953-1976 (New York: Harcourt Brace Jovanovich, 1976),
118-119. Wilbur, "The Bottles Become New, Too," in *Responses*, 215-223

[9]In the text and notes I will use the following abbreviations to refer to two major
collections of Richard Wilbur's writing: *NCP: New and Collected Poems* (San Diego,
New York, London: Harcourt Brace Jovanovich, 1988) and *R: Responses; Prose Pieces
1953-1976* (New York: Harcourt Brace Jovanovich, 1976). Each reference to a Wilbur
poem will also indicate the volume in which it first appeared: *BC: The Beautiful Changes
and Other Poems* (New York: Reynal and Hitchcock, 1947); *C: Ceremony and Other
Poems.* (New York: Harcourt, Brace, and Company, 1950); *TTW: Things of This
World; Poems by Richard Wilbur* (New York: Harcourt, Brace, and Co., 1956); *AP:
Advice to a Prophet and other poems* (New York: Harcourt, Brace and World, Inc.,
1961); *WS: Walking to Sleep; New Poems and Translations* (New York: Harcourt, Brace
and World, Inc., 1969); and *MR: The Mind-Reader; New Poems by Richard Wilbur*(New
York: Harcourt Brace Jovanovich, 1976).

characteristics they were revolting against. They have come to resemble the establishment. The new poetry has lost its freshness, he seems to say, having developed its own shallow conformities, its own rigid formulae for successful poems and successful poets. "Flippancies" has two parts, the first entitled, "The Star System":

> While you're a white hot youth, emit the rays
> Which, now unmarked, shall dazzle future days.
> Burn for the joy of it and waste no juice
> On hopes of prompt discovery. Produce!
>
> Then, white with years, live wisely and survive.
> Thus, you may be on hand when you arrive,
> And, like Antares, rosily dilate,
> And for a time be gaseous and great.

"The Star System" gains satiric force from its marvelously constructed astronomical conceit, from the use of the imperative (which lends this poem the tone of a poetical "Dear Abby" column), and from the humorous twists given to clichéd images of the artist. The cliché behind stanza one is drawn from Romanticism and has the artist driven to create by an irresistible muse. The philistine public, being more concerned with fame and fortune than fine art, ignores the artist and by its callous disregard consigns him to desolation and poverty. In "The Star System," however, it is the poet who is concerned with fame (fortune is added in part 2: "What's Good for the Soul Is Good for Sales"). The ostensibly passive instrument of the muse and victim of society is revealed to be active, calculating, shallow, and self-serving. In stanza two, the young poet survives to old age (contrary to the cliché which would have him stricken by consumption in the flower of youth or driven to suicide). "White with years," he takes on the role of sage. But this sage has nothing to say. He is interested only in reaping the harvest of his earlier efforts. Fame is a matter of arriving "gaseous and great" at the destination greedily anticipated as a youth.

Part 2 of "Flippancies" advises poets to make their fortunes by taking up the confessionalism of the new poetry:

If fictive music fails your lyre, confess-
Though not, of course, to any happiness.
So it be tristful, tell us what you choose:
Hangover, Nixon on the TV news,
God's death, the memory of your rocking horse,
Entropy, housework, Buchenwald, divorce,
Those damned flamingoes in your neighbor's yard. . .
All hangs together if you take it hard.

If poets are unable to handle "fictive music," the poem suggests that they consider cashing in on the popularity of confessional verse. The public's morbid fascination with poets' private miseries corresponds to the poets' indulgent self-pity. The result is book sales. Line three, "So it be tristful, tell us what you choose," is pivotal. When taken with the preceding lines, it reinforces the idea that public taste limits what these poets will say. When the line is grouped with those that follow, it forms a part of a proposal of openness to whatever happens to be in the poet's environment. But, choice cannot be avoided, and when the necessity to choose is not faced squarely, then all values are lost. One may juxtapose housework and Buchenwald, but the result will trivialize Buchenwald rather than elevate housework. The final line, "All hangs together if you take it hard" is double-edged. The pun centers on "hangs," and it includes the point being made about trivialization, that without discrimination everything loses its potential significance, being destroyed at once, all things "hanging" (by the neck until dead) together. The line also by implication reprehends solipsism for it ludicrously overstates the attitude that says that as long as I, the poet, can work up enough emotion over anything, it will hang together, that is, fit into my world. In Wilbur's view, reality is unavailable to one so self-centered, since it stands in its own right, no matter how the perceiver takes it.

This poem may be a flippancy, but it serves at least three serious purposes. It is a declaration of Wilbur's independence of literary fads. It implies his commitment to a poetry whose meaning is grounded outside the poet. And it exposes the ridiculousness of much of the negative criticism coming Wilbur's way.

Wilbur's reluctance to identify himself with some of the recently fashionable poetic programs and manifestos of his peers is grounded in his assessment of their relationship (and his) to their literary forebears. His most complete statement on this topic appears in an essay entitled, "On My Own Work."

> Another question often asked of the poets of my generation is where they stand in relation to the revolution in American poetry which is said to have begun in the second decade of this century. I think there truly *was* a revolution then . . . against trivial formalism, dead rhetoric, and genteel subject matter. The revolution was not a concerted one and there was little agreement on objectives. . . . But certainly it has been of lasting importance that Robinson and Frost chose to enliven traditional meters with the rhythms of colloquial speech; that Sandburg and others insisted on slang and on the brute facts of the urban and industrial scene; and that Pound and Eliot sophisticated American verse by introducing techniques from other literature, and by reviving and revising our sense of literary tradition.
>
> All of these contributions were inclusive and enlarging in character, but there were also, of course, experiments and movements of a reductive nature, in which one aspect of poetry was stressed at the expense of others. I think of Gertrude Stein's apparent efforts to reduce words to pure sound; . . . the typographical poems of Cummings, which–however engaging–sacrificed the ear to the eye; I think of the free verse movement which sought to purify poetry of all but organic rhythms; of the Imagist insistence that ideas be implicit in description, rather than abstractly stated; of the efforts of some poets to abandon logical progression and to write in quasimusical form. . . .
>
> My own position on poetry, if I have to have one, is that it should include every resource which can be made to work. . . . As a poet, my relationship to the revolution in question is that I am the grateful inheritor of all that my talent can employ, but that I will not accept any limitations or prohibitions or exclude anything in the name of purity. So far as possible, I try to play the whole instrument. (*R* 122-3)

Here Wilbur recasts the whole debate within American poetry and poetics whose terms had been set by the publication in 1960 of Donald Allen's *The New American Poetry*. As Allen himself states in the preface, the "one common characteristic" of the anthologized poets is their "total rejection of all those qualities typical of academic verse."[10] Wilbur's work is not found in this landmark collection, and his name is not associated with the

---

[10]Donald Allen, ed., *The New American Poetry* (New York: Grove Press, Inc., 1960), xi.

Black Mountain or San Francisco or Beat or New York or even Miscellaneous Writers whom Allen identifies as the "third generation" of twentieth century American poets. (Williams, Pound, H.D., Moore, Cummings, and Stevens are listed as the first generation; and in the second: Bishop, Lowell, Denby, Rexroth, and Zukofsky). I suspect, however, that Wilbur's attempt to recast the debate came less out of pique at his own exclusion from the emerging canon and more from his rejection of Allen's revisionist history of American poetry in this century. After all, how could any list of the dominant and influential figures of the "first generation" leave out T.S. Eliot, E.A. Robinson, John Crowe Ransom and Robert Frost? Or how could any list of the "second generation" ignore Theodore Roethke, John Berryman, Allen Tate, and Robert Penn Warren?

Wilbur's statement presents a far different view of things. He states that there "truly was" a "revolution in American poetry" in the second decade of this century, implying that subsequent claims to revolution are overstated. He drives home this point by identifying the poetic revolution of the second decade of the century as having been against "trivial formalism, dead rhetoric, and genteel subject matter," thus making the manifestos of the fifties and sixties sound like echoes rather than bold and original pronouncements. Furthermore, Wilbur subtly implies that, when his peers shifted from reacting against "academic verse" toward articulating their own goals, again there were precedents in the first half of the century. Wilbur's comment that Robinson and Frost had enlivened "traditional meters with the rhythms of colloquial speech" implies precedent for at least part of what mid-century poets were after in their "quest for immediacy."[11] Sandburg's "brute facts of the urban and industrial scene" can be seen as anticipating Charles Olson's "objectism" and his call for a profound respect for the independent reality of that which is outside the poet.[12] The freedom in relation to traditional forms exercised by Ezra Pound and the younger T.S. Eliot as they were "reviving and revising our sense of literary tradition" can be seen as antecedent to the

---

[11]James E. B. Breslin, *From Modern to Contemporary: American Poetry 1945-1965* (Chicago: The University of Chicago Press, 1984), xv.

[12]Charles Olson, "Projective Verse," in *The Poetics of the New American Poetry*, ed. Donald Allen and Warren Tallman (New York: Grove Press, Inc., 1973), 155-156.

longing for freedom expressed by poets in the fifties and sixties. Thus, the exemplary achievements from early twentieth century American poetry chosen by Wilbur for this list are brilliantly suited to undercut claims to originality made by polemicists in the mid-century debate. Finally, Wilbur lists a series of "experiments and movements of a reductive nature" (Stein, Cummings, free verse, imagism, and "the efforts of some poets to abandon logical progression and to write in quasimusical form"). In each case, the experiment reduces the role of rationality. And when Wilbur declares, "I will not accept any limitations or prohibitions or exclude anything in the name of purity," he is at once protecting the traditional role of the intellect and implying that in poetry it is not necessary to eliminate rationality in order to elevate into prominence what is visual, aural, respiratory, musical, sub- and unconscious.

Indeed, I believe that Wilbur's own great experiment involved wedding a "revolutionary" concern for holistic poetry with the New Critics' concern for poetic form. Though he does not say so explicitly, I think that this is what Wilbur meant when he wrote (early in his career):

> As regards technique, a critic has called me one of the "New Formalists," and I will accept the label provided it be understood that to try to revive the force of rhyme and other formal devices, by reconciling them with the experimental gains of the past several decades, is itself sufficiently experimental. [13]

His contribution to the debate, in other words, is an affair of his seeing the innovations of the fifties in the context of the previous half-century and of his producing a poetry which draws on this entire inheritance.

A still broader perspective that is compatible with Wilbur's comments would suggest that the mid-century debate about formal poetry is a continuance of an old Romantic debate and is traceable to differences between Coleridge and Wordsworth.[14]   By different means, Coleridge and

---

[13]Quoted in *Twentieth Century Authors, First Supplement*, ed. Stanley Kunitz (New York: The R.W. Wilson Co., 1966), 1080.

[14]Charles Altieri, "From Symbolist Thought to Immanence: The Ground of Postmodern American Poetics," *Boundary 2* 1, 3 (Spring 1973), 607.

Wordsworth sought to overcome the disjunction between mind and world that was perceived by Newtonian physics and Kantian epistemology. On the one hand, Coleridge promoted the notion that the human mind ought to be relied on to create an order connecting subject and object.[15] The younger Wordsworth, on the other hand, relied on a reality outside his own mind to overcome the mind / world dichotomy. He wrote of "a presence . . . a sense sublime / Of something . . . deeply interfused / A motion and a spirit, that impels / All thinking things . . . / And rolls through all things."[16] And when contemporary American poetry is seen to be the heir to these two varieties of Romanticism, we may then trace one line of development forward from Wordsworth to Emerson to Whitman to D.H. Lawrence, and to William Carlos Williams and Roethke and on to such "postmoderns" as Charles Olson, Robert Bly, and Robert Duncan. The other line goes from Coleridge to the Symbolists to Yeats, Eliot, Pound, Crane, and Stevens.[17] Charles Altieri charges that, after Stevens, American Romanticism deriving from Coleridge

> narrows into the academic criticism of second-generation New Critics and the attenuated verbal artifice characteristic of poetry in the 1950s. The central commitment of this tradition is to the creative, form-giving imagination and its power to affect society, or at least personal needs for meaning, by constructing coherent, fully human forms out of the flux of experience.[18]

---

[15]However, Gerald Graff believes that the logical consequences of Coleridge's ideas "furthered the loss of community they were seeking to redress." Graff's essay, "The Myth of the Postmodern Breakthrough," contends that Coleridge, virtually the whole Romantic tradition, and even our most recent poets are understood best as exemplifying the influence of Kant's philosophy, rather than carrying on a rebellion against it: "The romantic Absolute degenerates into a myth or, as we now say, a fiction." Gerald Graff, *Literature Against Itself: Literary Ideas in Modern Society* (Chicago: University of Chicago Press, 1979), 39.

[16]"Lines Composed a Few Miles Above Tintern Abbey," lines 94-102

[17]Altieri, "From Symbolist Thought . . ." 607. Altieri, *Enlarging the Temple: New Directions in American Poetry during the 1960s* (London: Associated University Presses, Inc., 1979), 17. Ekbert Faas, *Towards a New American Poetics: Essays and Interviews* (Santa Barbara: Black Sparrow Press, 1979), 41.

[18]Altieri, *Enlarging the Temple*, 17.

According to Altieri, it was the resurgence of Wordsworthian Romanticism which revitalized American poetry in the fifties and sixties.

But, however one responds to Altieri's judgment, it should be clear that a sufficiently spacious historical perspective will prompt some skepticism about the conclusions of those who differentiate sharply between Wilbur's work and the "new American poetry" of his time. There *are* differences between Wilbur and O'Hara, Olson, Merwin, and Levertov (to name a few), but there are also important similarities which ought to be noted in balanced assessments of Wilbur's work. For example, most commentators on American poetry agree that a common goal of the various innovative poetic movements of the fifties and sixties was the desire they all had to "capture immediacy."[19] Innovative poets hoped to reflect and evoke spontaneity with their writing. They tried to write a poetry which would overcome "the alienation of man from his body and his unconscious, from others, and from his environment."[20] These are certainly restatements of the Romantic quest for overcoming the dichotomy of subject and object. And surely, if writers as diverse as Wordsworth and Coleridge, Lawrence and Hopkins, Williams and Eliot may all be said to have participated in that quest, there is room for Allen Ginsberg, James Merrill, and Richard Wilbur also.

Wilbur's commitment to immediacy has been constantly kept throughout his career. In the early poem "Objects" (*BC:NCP* 360-1), for example, his description of the painting "A Dutch Courtyard" by Pieter de Hooch accomplishes that which the poem calls for in its more didactic sections. Wilbur urges his readers to avoid abstractions and to "have objects speak." Then, the painting is presented and it, as it were, is allowed to speak: Wilbur's words recreate the eyes' movements as they are drawn from one part of the painting to another:

> . . . see feinting from his plot of paint
> The trench of light on boards, the much-mended dry
> Courtyard wall of brick,

---

[19] Breslin, xv, 30, 61. Altieri, *Enlarging the Temple*, 37, 128. Faas, 9-12.

[20] Altieri, *Enlarging the Temple*, 34.

> And sun submerged in beer, and streaming in glasses,
> The weave of a sleeve, the careful and undulant tile.

Wilbur's evocation corresponds marvelously to the experience of viewing "A Dutch Courtyard," which hangs in The National Gallery of Art, Washington, D.C. In "Love Calls Us to the Things of This World" (*TTW:NCP* 233) readers also feel present when "the eyes open to a cry of pulleys"; or when in "A Fire Truck" (*AP:NCP* 207), "Redness, brass, ladders and hats hurl past, / Blurring to sheer verb." Wilbur's poetical address to insomniacs, "Walking to Sleep" (*WS:NCP* 158-61), captures immediacy as an address to all who are journeying toward death (for which sleep is the metaphor). Wilbur heightens the poem's tone of immediacy by engaging his readers in a series of mental exercises. The poem resembles a guided meditation:

> As a queen sits down, knowing that a chair will be there,
> Or a general raises his hand and is given the field-glasses,
> Step off assuredly into the blank of your mind:
> Something will come to you. Although at first
> You nod through nothing like a fogbound prow,
> Gravel will breed in the margins of your gaze,
> Perhaps with tussocks or a dusty flower,
> And, humped like dolphins playing in the bow-wave,
> Hills will suggest themselves. All such suggestions
> Are yours to take or leave, but hear this warning:
> Let them not be too velvet green, the fields
> . . . (etc.)

The appeal of his theme, the use of direct address, and the dialogical format all conspire with Wilbur's arresting images and technical mastery of rhythm and diction to make this a poem to be experienced, rather than a poem about experience. Wilbur, like so many of his peers, is a poet of "immediacy."

Wilbur also shares his generation's devotion to the things of this world. By and large contemporary poets look outside themselves to find reality or else so deeply within that they discover a reality that is transpersonal, as have

Romantic poets from Wordsworth to Charles Olson.[21] Even the followers of Coleridge who place relatively more importance on the constructive imagination most often recognize the distinct objectivity of reality outside the mind.[22] It is, after all, the mind's task (in Coleridge's thought) to overcome the disjunction between subject and object, rather than to deny objective reality. Both Wilbur and the poets with whom critics contrast his work stand clearly within this admittedly broad tradition. Wilbur calls for "devoutness" in the face of alterity, an attitude which recognizes that "Love Calls Us to the Things of This World" (the title of his most celebrated poem, *TTW:NCP* 233-4).[23]

But, though Wilbur shares the concern of his contemporaries to bridge the gap between self and world and pay the world reverential attention, he and they differ in their perceptions of the utility of poetry's formal elements in pursuit of their common goals.[24] Wilbur believes formal

---

[21]In "Tintern Abbey," Wordsworth wrote that "nature and the language of sense" were "the nurse / The guide, the guardian of my heart." Charles Olson advocated "projective verse" by which he sought to "listen . . . [to the] secrets objects share." Olson, 152, 156.

[22]Wilbur, himself, has made this point nicely in his essay, "Poetry and Happiness": "One does not think of Wallace Stevens, who so stressed the transforming power of imagination, as having much in common with Frost, and yet Stevens would agree that the best and happiest dreams of the poet are those that involve no denial of the fact. In his poem 'Crude Foyer,' Stevens acknowledges that poets are tempted to turn inward and conceive an interior paradise, but that is a false happiness. . . . We cannot be content, we cannot enjoy poetic happiness, until the inner paradise is brought to terms with the world before us, and our vision fuses with the view from the window." (*R* 104-105)

[23]In his article, "The Bottles Become New, Too" (*R* 215-223), Wilbur links his own "devoutness" toward the world with attitudes expressed in the writings of Marianne Moore, William Carlos Williams, James Agee, and others. I believe it also resembles what Heidegger means by *Gelassenheit*, as explained in Nathan Scott's essay on the poetry of Theodore Roethke. See *The Wild Prayer of Longing* (New Haven: Yale University Press, 1971), especially the second and third chapters. Charles Altieri (*Enlarging the Temple*, 225) follows Scott's lead and identifies O'Hara, Snyder, Creely, and Merwin as postmodern poets who "each give resonance and imaginative life to Heideggerean claims." Wilbur, too, ought to be included in this list.

[24]This is, however, a relative and not absolute distinction. The *avant-garde* used poetry's formal elements as they experimented. In practice, their poems are sometimes not much different than Wilbur's in this regard. Mid-century American poets present a whole

poetry may evoke realities that are dynamic or static, chaotic or orderly, mysterious or obvious. Most of the *avant-garde* agreed with Allen Tate's conclusion that formal verse has a more limited usefulness: "Formal versification is the primary structure of poetic order, the assurance to the reader and to the poet himself that the poet is in control of the disorder both outside him and within his own mind."[25] So, as the *avant-garde* sought to *lose* control in order to gain breadth and depth of vision, strict adherence to formal conventions seemed counterproductive. Robert Duncan is typical of those who have felt confined by the dogmatism they took to be a part of the poetics of New Criticism:

> Against the Gnostics, who would free the sparks of the Spirit from what is the matter, and against the positivists and semanticists who would free the matter from its inspirational chaos, I am glad that there is a night and day, Heaven and Hell, love and wrath, sanity and ecstasie, together in a little place. . . . What I most abhor [is] what most seems to exclude or mistake the exuberance of my soul. . . . Form to the mind obsessed by convention, is significant insofar as it shows control. . . . It is a magic that still survives in Christian Science and the New Criticism, a magic that removes the reasonable thing from its swarming background of unreason-unmentionable areas where all the facts that reason cannot regulate are excluded and appear as error, savage tribes, superstitions and anarchical mobs, passions, madnesses, enthusiasms, and bad manners. . . . Poets who once had dreams and epiphanies, now admit only to devices and ornaments.[26]

Later in the same essay, Duncan differentiates between those who use form to control and those, such as Marianne Moore and Robert Lowell, who

---

spectrum of degrees of reliance on traditional sonic and metric practices. See the essays by Daniel Hoffman, "Poetry: After Modernism," "Poetry: Schools of Dissidents," and "Poetry: Dissidents from Schools," in the *Harvard Guide to Contemporary American Writing*, ed. Daniel Hoffman (Cambridge: The Belknap Press of Harvard University Press, 1979), especially pp. 486, 492-3, 512, 532, 556-7, 576. As poets talk or write about poetry, the lines are more sharply drawn, and Wilbur's defense of traditional poetic forms is quite different from what one reads in essays by his most prestigious peers.

[25]Tate, "Poetry Modern and Unmodern," in *Essays of Four Decades* (Chicago, 1968), 228. Quoted in Breslin, 28.

[26]Robert Duncan, "Ideas of the Meaning of Form," in Allen and Tallman, 195-197.

use form "along lines . . . of a psychic need." He is not against using form *per se*, but against imposing form on vitality rather than allowing form to arise from it.[27] It is Duncan's kind of passionate revolt against whatever might limit his experience that has raised suspicions that, with all Wilbur's skill as a craftsman and control over his medium, he limits the reality to which he has access. And, of course, he himself has written about poetry as a way of keeping chaos under control:

> It was not until World War II took me to Cassino, Anzio and the Siegfried Line that I began to versify in earnest. One does not use poetry for its major purposes, as a means of organizing oneself and the world, until one's world somehow gets out of hand.[28]

This passage has been used to illustrate Wilbur's preoccupation with order, but it ought not to be taken out of its context. The paragraph in which it appears concludes: "Poetry, to be vital, does seem to need a periodic acquaintance with the threat of Chaos." And this sentence suggests what is indeed the thesis of this book, that Richard Wilbur remains dedicated to formal discipline precisely *because* it is capable of moving beyond order to evoke the threat of chaos, vitality, mystery, and transcendence. By means of their carefully constructed tensions in rhyme, rhythm, imagery, and diction, Wilbur's poems spring beyond conventional lyricism. "His work," says Anthony Hecht, "is the most kinetic poetry I know."[29] Indeed, it is through the movement of his poems that Wilbur discloses his most fundamental poetic, philosophic, and religious commitments.

The importance of movement in Wilbur's poems is everywhere apparent. Sometimes it is made obvious by their titles-as, for example, "Love Calls Us to the Things of This World" (*TTW:NCP* 233-4), "Water Walker" (*BC:NCP* 338-41), "Walking to Sleep" (*WS:NCP* 158-61), "On The Marginal Way" (*WS:NCP* 120-2), and "Running" (*WS:NCP* 137-9).

---

[27] Duncan, 201.

[28] *Twentieth Century Authors*, 1079-80.

[29] Anthony Hecht, "The Motions of the Mind," in Salinger, 123.

Moreover, there are poems in which motion is meticulously analyzed or described: "Grace" (*BC:NCP* 384-5), "A Grasshopper" (*AP:NCP* 202-3), "Juggler" *(C:NCP* 297), "The Writer" (*MR:NCP* 53-4), and "An Event" (*TTW:NCP* 274). Even poems about plants are filled with images of movement:

> Those laden lilacs
>> at the lawn's end
> Came stark, spindly,
>> and in staggered file,
> Like walking wounded
>> from the dead of winter.

> ("The Lilacs," *WS:NCP* 118-19)

> The ferns . . .
> Will climb through timber as a smoking tide . . .
> And, wave on wave, like some green infantry,
> Storm all the slope as high as eye can see.

> ("Fern-Beds in Hampshire County," *WS:NCP* 125-6)

Even the sight "Of layered rock two miles above my head" prompts a reverie about how it once "Hove ages up and broke / Soundless asunder" as a result of shrinkage in the "skin / Of Earth" ("On the Marginal Way" *WS:NCP* 120-2). Furthermore, mind and spirit are consistently moving in Wilbur's poems and the images he chooses to depict them are vital and kinetic.

The opening lines of "Part of a Letter" offer a typical example of Wilbur's kineticism:[30]

> Easy as cove water rustles its pebbles and shells
> In the slosh, spread, seethe, and the backsliding
> Wallop and tuck of the wave, and just that cheerful,
>> Tables and earth were riding

---

[30]My analysis of these lines is an expansion of Clive James's brief but suggestive comment in which he states that they show Wilbur possessing a "mastery of mimesis." James, in Salinger, 109.

Back and forth in the minting shades of the trees.

(*C:NCP* 286)

The first three lines are onomatopoeic in sound and perfectly timed in rhythm. The *s* sounds ("ru*s*tle*s* it*s* pebble*s* and *s*hell*s*") genuinely rustle and work in part because they conjure up aural memories of the reader's own visits to cove water. The "slosh, spread, seethe" of line two brings to mind the way water moves around, over, and through the sand and rocks of the shoreline. As the water recedes, our imagining eye is taken from the minute particularity of this shell and that pebble to the larger motion of the wave. Our field of vision, hearing, and awareness is enlarged even further as the retreating wave is met by its incoming successor, and we hear in the end sounds of wall*op* and tu*ck* the slap of water on water. All that movement, so vividly presented, is then made to serve another image. Just as the sea moves, so, too, do the tables and floor of the outdoor cafe, as they appear to be "riding / Back and forth in the minting shades of the trees." The choice of the rather odd word "minting" (meaning both "fabricating" this imaginative idea that tables can move, *and* "making a threatening gesture or movement"- *O.E.D.*) confirms our suspicion that our imagination has been transported from a child-like fascination with the seashore to a threatening and unsettling mystery. If tables are insubstantial and the earth moves, we have lost our bearings; vertigo has set in. By means of his great skill with the formal elements of poetry, Wilbur has, in this poem's first five lines, described key aspects of two dynamic scenes with keen precision, and he has also stimulated his readers' memories and imaginations, taking them from the known to the unknown, from daydream to nightmare.

"Teresa" (*MR:NCP* 79) not only moves the reader away from order toward vitality as effectively as "Part of a Letter", it is also *about* the relationship of order and ecstasy. The poem implies that, as disciplined prayer led to spiritual transport in the life of St. Teresa, so, too, discipline may lead to transport in poetry:

> After the sun's eclipse,
> The brighter angel and the spear which drew

A bridal outcry from her open lips,
　　She could not prove it true,
Nor think at first of any means to test
By what she had been wedded or possessed.

　　Not all cries were the same;
There was an island in mythology
Called by the very vowels of her name
　　Where vagrants of the sea,
Changed by a wand, were made to squeal and cry
As heavy captives in a witch's sty.

　　The proof came soon and plain:
Visions were true which quickened her to run
God's barefoot errands in the rocks of Spain
　　Beneath its beating sun,
And lock the O of ecstasy within
The tempered consonants of discipline.

In "Teresa" Wilbur generously makes use of formal regularity. There are six lines in each stanza, a regular syllabic pattern (6 10 10 6 10 10), a regular pattern of stresses (3 4 4 3 4 4), and the end rhymes are patterned *ababcc*. Almost every line is held together sonically, sometimes by assonance ("prove / true"; "came / plain") and sometimes by alliteration ("*v*ery *v*owels . . . *w*and, *w*ere"). There are other repetitions of important sounds, such as the *s* of "*s*un's eclip*s*e" and the open vowel sounds of "*A* bridal outcry from her open lips" in the poem's opening lines. And in the poem's closing lines there is the superb joining of sound and sense as "the O of ecstasy" is followed by "The tempered consonants of discipline." Though tempered, the power of the penultimate line lingers over the last, and the idea of discipline does not seem to "lock" up ecstasy in any way that would suggest diminishment of its freedom.

The relationship of order and ecstasy is also addressed in several of Wilbur's allusions in "Teresa." For example, the marriage imagery of stanza one ("bridal," line 3, "wedded," line 6) comes straight from the common vocabulary of mystical writings in Teresa's time.[31] The "brighter angel and the spear" (line 2) refer to a particular vision of St. Teresa's known as the "Transverberation of the Heart." At the climax of the vision, an angel plunged a flaming golden spear into her heart: "It was, as it were, the orgasm of the mystic nuptials."[32] Then in stanza three, these ecstatic visions are revealed to have occurred in the context of disciplined prayer. The word "barefoot" ("Visions were true which quickened her to run / God's barefoot errands in the rocks of Spain") alludes to "discalced," a term applied to monastic orders, symbolically indicating their dedication to the poor. "Discalced" literally means barefoot or unshod. St. Teresa's mystical visions led her to found several convents patterned after the model of the Discalced Franciscans. In this context, then, the allusion to Teresa's "barefoot errands" may refer both to humble acts of charity and to the founding of institutions which fostered disciplined contemplation, contemplation which could lead to experiences of glorious and mystical transport. Even this rather obscure allusion contributes to the marriage of ecstasy and discipline toward which the poem is moving.

The "O" of ecstasy (line 5, stanza three) refers to the groan Teresa uttered during the "Transverberation of the Heart." Wilbur may have had in mind the shape of Teresa's mouth in Bernini's sculpture of this incident, located in the Cornaro Chapel in Rome. Robert T. Petersson provides not only a description of the statue, but also a greater understanding of the not so subtle eroticism of Teresa's experience (and of Wilbur's poem):

> The face is idealized yet strongly sensuous. Of the erotic quality so often commented on, fleeting signs are visible in the hands and feet, in the contours of the mouth, chin, and brow. . . . Unquestionably the figure of Teresa is erotic, but in no exclusively physical sense. . . . Not until recent centuries has it been necessary to explain that in genuine religious ecstasy body, mind, and spirit are all involved. . . . In union Teresa's human and

---

[31] Stephen Clissold, *St. Teresa of Avila* (London: Sheldon Press, 1979), 66.

[32] Clissold, 60.

divine natures both belong to God. Teresa's moment of ecstasy looks to the resurrection of body and spirit alike.[33]

In Teresa's story, Wilbur has found precedent for the holistic and ecstatic experience so eagerly sought by his generation of poets. But, unlike so many of them, Wilbur expresses and evokes ecstatic experience by relying on the structures of traditional verse and allusions of a decidedly intellectual cast.

Equally intellectual is another allusion in "Teresa." ("There was an island in mythology / Called by the very vowels of her name.") It is a reference to Circe's island, Aeaea, which Odysseus visited in the course of his journey homeward to Ithaca from the Trojan War. To skeptics and to Teresa herself in moments of doubt, the question arose as to whether her transports might not have more in common with sorcery or witchcraft than with genuine religious experience. Just as the companions of Odysseus were entrapped by Circe's witchcraft, Teresa's mysticism at times seemed more like the entrapment of illusion than the fruit of contemplation. The question of her visions' authenticity is first presented in stanza one, "She could not prove [her vision] true, / Nor think at first of any means to test / By what she had been wedded or possessed." This question is carried through the allusion in stanza two with significant metrical acceleration. Stanza three is magnificent in its return to solid-sounding verse. The heavy *p* sounds of line one ("The proof came soon and plain") slow the poem down as if to reassure the reader that an answer to Teresa's question is at hand. However, the answer is not given in the same terms in which the questions were asked. The proof of visionary authenticity is not testable in any scientific way, but it comes in the kind of spirituality the visions inspire. In Teresa's case, it was a spirituality which called her to a life of prayer, charity, contemplation, and openness to

---

[33]Robert T. Petersson, *The Art of Ecstasy: Teresa, Bernini, and Crashaw* (London: Routledge & Kegan Paul, 1970), 72-3. It is not unusual to find conjunctions of the spiritual and the sexual in Wilbur's poems. Other quite obvious examples would include "John Chapman" (*MR:NCP* 77), "Children of Darkness" (*MR:NCP* 80-1), "A Wedding Toast" (*MR:NCP* 61), and "The Writer" (*MR:NCP* 53-4), all from Wilbur's sixth book of poems. Though evidence of sexuality can be found in Wilbur's early work, too (see, e.g., the title poem of his first volume, *The Beautiful Changes*), it is in his later work that more explicit sexual images are used and a more central role assigned to them.

visions which could be cultivated by adherence to strict monastic standards of discipline.

Wilbur's employment of poetry's formal resources in both "Teresa" and "Part of a Letter" move the poems into realms of mystery and spirituality. We are taken from our normal world of sense perceptions ("Part of a Letter") and conventional thought (the desire to "prove" the truth of visionary experience in "Teresa") to realms in which the ordinary is charged with a new and surprising significance. It is my contention that many of Wilbur's poems are poems of similar motions.

Chapter Two

INTUITIONS OF THE SPIRIT IN AN IMPERFECT WORLD

When I play the critic to my work, as I am doing now, it is not hard to see
. . . persistent concerns. The . . . poems I have included here all have to do
(a critic might say) with the proper relation between the tangible world and
the intuitions of the spirit. The poems assume that such intuitions are, or
may be, true; they incline, however, to favor a spirituality that is not
abstracted, not dissociated and world renouncing.

Richard Wilbur

His . . . poetry accepts the things of this world; it does not honor their
imperfections, as the poetry of a jejune optimist might; rather it celebrates
the ineffaceable beauty which subsists in an imperfect universe, a beauty
which is both created by imperfection and in adamant conflict with it.

John P. Farrell

There are risks of corruption, then, in becoming a poet-citizen rather than
an alienated artist, but I myself would consider them risks well taken,
because it seems to me that poetry is sterile unless it arises from a sense of
community. I think this is true even in America, where beneath so much
surface homogeneity there lies a radical commitment to diversity and to
the toleration of dissent. We are not a settled and monolithic nation. . . .
Yet the incoherence of America need not enforce a stance of alienation in
the poet; rather it may be seen as placing on him a peculiar imaginative
burden, and committing him perhaps to something like Yeats' long and
loyal quarrel with his native Ireland.

Richard Wilbur

That Richard Wilbur's poetry regularly explores spiritual realities incarnate in the physical world has been noticed by some of his most sensitive critics. Peter Stitt entitles his essay, "The Sacramental Vision of Richard Wilbur." Ralph Mills rightly observes: "While it would be an exaggeration to call him a religious poet in any strict or doctrinal sense of the word, it is equally false not to recognize the fact that he is often concerned with an experience of life which can only be named religious." Anthony Hecht refers to Wilbur's "religious temper" and Paul F. Cummins points toward "an implicit Christian quality in Wilbur's thought."[1]

Wilbur himself has written that his poems reveal a "persistent concern" with the "proper relation between the tangible world and the intuitions of the spirit" (*R* 125). His concern repeatedly leads him to meditate on the character of that world and his own perceptual capabilities. He wonders whether the presence of evil makes a mockery of his predilection to give the world reverent attention. He ponders the proper role of the imagination in perception. He muses about his place in the public realm: what posture and action should he take in response to what he sees?

Some critics, assuming that poetic form inevitably functions as a means to keep chaos at bay,[2] have charged Wilbur with insensitivity to suffering and indifference to the evils of our time. They see his "religious temper" as insulation against unpleasantness. "How can he be so damnably good-natured in an abominable world?" asks Hyam Plutzik.[3] Cummins agrees that Wilbur "chooses to dwell on the beautiful," and then, in a misguided attempt to defend him, argues that Wilbur's sunny disposition is salutary for our age.[4] These assessments of Wilbur's work miss the mark.

---

[1]Peter Stitt, "The Sacramental Vision of Richard Wilbur," in *The World's Hieroglyphic Beauty: Five American Poets* (Athens, The University of Georgia Press, 1985), 9-38. Ralph Mills, "The Lyricism of Richard Wilbur," in Salinger (see chap. 1, n. 1), 80-81. Anthony Hecht, "The Motions of the Mind," in Salinger, 123. Paul F. Cummins, *Richard Wilbur: A Critical Essay*, Contemporary Writers in Christian Perspective (Grand Rapids: Wm. B. Eerdmans, 1971), 22.

[2]See Chapter One, 15-17.

[3]Hyam Plutzik, "Recent Poetry," in Salinger, 68.

[4]Cummins, 16-29.

They overlook his career-long commitment to seeing the world as it is, confronting head on this world's harshness as well as its beauty and grace. Indeed, his eye for beauty and grace has been sharpened by the haunting possibility that chaos is the world's fundamental condition. Encounters with evil give urgency to his quest for contact with some sort of benevolent transcendence.

In fact, more than twenty poems out of the eighty-five in Wilbur's first two collections are predominantly expressions of horror, despair, and disgust. His war poems, for example, express the darker side of his vision. One of them is "The Peace of Cities" (*BC:NCP* 351) in which the influence of the early Eliot[5] is apparent as the poem evokes an urban evening:

Terrible streets, the manichee hell of twilight
Glides like a giant bass between your windows,

Dark deploying in minnows into your alleys
Stirs and hushes the reefs of scudding trash.

Withinwalls voices, past the ports and locks,
Murmur below the shifting of crockery

I know not what; the barriered day expires
In scattered sounds of dread inconsequence.

This poem may be derivative, but it manages powerfully to suggest that the assumption that peace resides in our cities is an illusion. Dusk is portrayed as menacing by means of the baleful image of the giant bass gliding between windows. The "twilight hell" outside corresponds to the sinister vacuity of the domestic scenes inside. Those who "murmur below the shifting of crockery" are victims trapped in a meaningless routine that, in the rest of the poem, is said to be more destructive to the human spirit than even the devastations of war.

---

[5]See especially "The Love Song of J. Alfred Prufrock" in *The Complete Poems and Plays: 1909-1950* (New York: Harcourt, Brace & World, Inc., 1971), 3-7.

In "On The Eyes of an S.S. Officer" (*BC:NCP* 348), the officer manifests evil in an atmosphere as sinister as that evoked in "The Peace of Cities."

> I think of Amundsen, enormously bit
> By arch-dark flurries on the ice plateau,
> An amorist of violent virgin snows
> At the cold end of the world's spit.
>
> Or a Bombay saint asquat in the marketplace,
> Eyes gone from staring the sun over the sky,
> Who still dead-reckons that acetylene eye,
> An eclipsed mind in a blind face.
>
> But this one's iced or ashen eyes devise,
> Foul purities, in flesh their wilderness,
> Their fire; I ask my makeshift God of this
> My opulent bric-a-brac earth to damn his eyes.

Donald Hill claims that "the poem fails to rise to the unavoidable seriousness of its theme."[6] I disagree. As with Frost's "Fire and Ice," [7] this poem's apocalyptic meditation encompasses both personal and universal concerns. Here, the speaker has no solid ground on which to stand in judgment of the horror around himself. As he prays to his "makeshift God," he is as unable to resist the inexorable malevolence of the SS as Amundsen and the Bombay saint were to resist the forces of nature. I'm not sure how Wilbur's poem could be any more serious than it is.

Wilbur's later work, too, can be vivid in its portrayal of malignity in the human condition. The ennui of our age certainly comes through many of

---

[6]Donald L. Hill, *Richard Wilbur* (New York: Twayne Publishers, Inc., 1967), 22-23.

[7]"Fire and Ice" in *The Poetry of Robert Frost*, ed. Edward Connery Lathem (New York: Holt, Rinehart and Winston, 1969), 220.

Wilbur's translations, particularly those from Voznesensky.[8] Crass greed is the subject of "Matthew VIII, 28 ff." (*WS:NCP* 154). The sinister side of sexuality is present in "Piccola Comedia" (*MR:NCP* 59-60), "Children of Darkness" (*MR:NCP* 80-1), and "John Chapman" (*MR:NCP* 77). "John Chapman" also makes a broader statement about humanity's propensity to evil by alluding to Scripture as a way of communicating key elements of Wilbur's own vision. Here the references to *Genesis* and its myths of the creation and fall let us know that Wilbur is telling John Chapman's story within a world view that sees evil as a tragic corruption of original goodness, a corruption that cannot easily be reversed. The first two stanzas of "John Chapman" verge on being a parody of Freudian symbolism:

> Beside the Brokenstraw or Licking Creek,
> Wherever on the virginal frontier
> New men with rutting wagons came to seek
> Fresh paradises for the axe to clear,
>
> John Chapman fostered in a girdled glade
> Or river-flat new apples for their need,
> Till half the farmsteads of the west displayed
> White blossoms sprung of his authentic seed.

John Chapman (Johnny Appleseed) is one of many figures in lore and literature who fit the pattern discerned by R.W.B. Lewis, the pattern of an American Adam in an Edenic wilderness. Adopting Lewis' categories for a moment, it is possible to see this poem as descending from the nineteenth century's literature of "ironic temperament" which "was characterized by a tragic optimism: by a sense of the tragic collisions to which innocence was liable." However, the odds against Chapman's innocence coming to fruition are so great that the poem almost slips into another category, that of the

---

[8]Three of Wilbur's translations of poems by Voznesensky are included in *Walking to Sleep* and two more in *The Mind-Reader*. In "Poetry's Debt to Poetry," Wilbur wrote: "One thing that moves a poet to translate from other tongues, as I know from my own experience, is the urge to broaden his utterance through imposture, to say things he is not yet able to say in his own person." (*R* 169)

"party of memory" to whom "the sinfulness of man seemed never so patent as currently in America."[9] To be sure, Chapman was a man of faith: "trusting in God, mistrusting artifice, / He would not graft or bud the stock he sold." But, the poem asks, "what, through nature's mercy, came of this?" The answer is harsh. His faith begat

> . . . the old *malus malus*, double-dyed
> Eurasia's wilding since the bitter fall,
> Sparse upon branches as perplexed as pride,
> An apple gnarled, acidulous, and small.

What comes of trusting God and nature's mercy is "evil, evil" and double death. Fruit is sparse, tough, bitter and small that grows on twisted, tangled branches as "perplexed as pride." The poem ends with an invocation of John Chapman's spirit, offered as a gesture toward hope without any expectation that practical gain will come of it.

> Out of your grave, John Chapman, in Fort Wayne,
> May you arise, and flower, and come true.
> We meanwhile, being of a spotted strain
> And born into a wilder land than you,
>
> Expecting less of natural tree or man
> And dubious of working out the brute,
> Affix such hopeful scions as we can
> To the rude, forked, and ever savage root.

In a note, Wilbur informs us, "With few exceptions, apple trees raised from the seed of cultivated varieties do not 'come true,' but revert to the wild Eurasian type" (*MR:NCP* 112). In other words, since John Chapman's trust and service were aberrations from the norm of fallen humanity, when his spirit is invoked one ought not expect it to "come true." Furthermore, "we" acknowledge that all attempts at cultivation, civilization, and refinement have not cleansed us of our "spotted strain." America is now an even "wilder land"

---

[9] R.W.B. Lewis, *The American Adam: Innocence, Tragedy, and Tradition in the Nineteenth Century* (Chicago: The University of Chicago Press, Phoenix Books, 1955), 7.

than when it was being settled. One can only conclude that remembering John Chapman is futile–a rather pathetic attempt to "affix such hopeful scions as we can."

Wilbur's references to the drama of Eden in "John Chapman" are not unusual. He broods on the loss of innocence in scores of poems,[10] many of which allude to the Biblical account of the fall. However, Wilbur does not always conclude with the pessimism expressed in "John Chapman." Indeed, he often seems to be embracing something like a doctrine of the "fortunate fall": that is, as a consequence of humanity's struggle with evil, such virtues emerge as honesty, courage, and openness to grace. He seems to believe that a fall from innocence may make one more spiritually aware rather than less.

In "A Problem from Milton" (*C:NCP* 311), Wilbur speculates on what might have led Adam to commit his fateful sin:

> In Eden palm and open-handed pine
> Displayed to God and man their flat perfection.
> Carefully coiled, the regulation vine
> Submitted to our general sire's inspection.
>
> And yet the streams in mazy error went;
> Powdery flowers a potent odor gave;
> The trees, on second thoughts, were lushly blent
> And swashed forever like a piling wave.
>
> The builded comber like a hurdling horse
> Achieves the rocks. With wild informal roar
> The spray upholds its freedom and its force,
> But leaves the limpet and the whelk ashore.
>
> In spirals of the whelk's eternal shell
> The mind of Swedenborg to heaven flew,

---

[10]Some representative titles are, "A Problem From Milton" (*C:NCP* 311), "Then" (*C:NCP* 281), "The Pardon" (*C:NCP* 285), "Mined Country" (*BC:NCP* 343-4), "Under Cygnus" (*WS:NCP* 140), and "Merlin Enthralled" (*TTW:NCP* 245-6).

> But found it such a mathematic hell
> That Emerson was damned if it would do.
>
> Poor Adam, deviled by your energy,
> What power egged you on to feed your brains?
> Envy the gorgeous gallop of the sea,
> Whose horses never know their lunar reins.

The poem wants, of course, to suggest how inadequately "flat perfection" (stanza one) describes the sheer amplitude of the natural order, since everywhere there is potency and vitality–the unpredictable course of streams, intoxicating floral odors, and the ocean's "wild informal roar." The world is filled with a kind of glorious excess: things spill across boundaries and defy explanations. Perhaps, this poem hypothesizes, Adam, too, was created with a tendency to ignore boundaries. He was "deviled" by his "energy," "egged . . . on to feed [his] brains" by vitality within. The reader is left asking why the Creator would punish Adam so severely for being true to his created nature. The last two stanzas say *that* is a mystery, unfathomed by even so mathematic a mind as Swedenborg's.

Adam's fallen condition leads to the ironic suggestion (in the poem's final lines) that it would be better for Adam if he did not know the fall was God's fault. Perhaps Adam ought to envy nature which doesn't have the capacity to know why it acts as it does: "Envy the gorgeous gallops of the sea, / Whose horses never know their lunar reigns." But finally the poem's implied conclusion is that even though the last problem is serious, it is more fortunate that humankind should be moved by all sorts of vaulting ambitions than that we should represent merely "flat perfection."

"For Ellen" (*BC:NCP* 388) is concerned with one of the benefits that derives from the loss of innocence, a new way of seeing the world. Wilbur muses on the child Ellen's attempts to see what is real and true while she swings in mood from nightmarish fright to the bright "blue heal-all" outlook of a Pollyanna. He promises her maturity, a "starker sight," similar to that which is the basis for Wilbur's own religious vision:

> But sometimes you will look at the lazy sun
> Hammocked in clouds, dead-slumbering in the sky.

> The casual fire will blister blue, and night
> Will strand its fears; then with a starker sight
> And newer darker love, you will supply
> The world of joy which never was begun.

The fall from innocence here is characterized as a cleansing process. Afterwards Ellen will no longer distort the threat of evil by exaggeration or repression. As Paul F. Cummins concludes:

> The Fall for Wilbur is not a blight; it is a fortunate event. For with sin, responsibility, and death, the Fall also brings about a "starker sight." And against the new awareness, the new tragic sense, life takes on far greater mystery and depth. The Fall occurs in time, but the love and joy born out of the Fall transcend time; this love and joy "never was begun."[11]

"Love and joy born out of the Fall" mark Wilbur's religious vision even when it focuses on death, the last extremity, as in "A Black November Turkey" (*TTW:NCP* 238-9). There, Wilbur shows that his vision is capacious enough to include in one poem both his tragic sense and a profound delight in life's mystery and depth.

> Nine white chickens come
> With haunchy walk and heads
> Jabbing among the chips, the chaff, the stones
> And the cornhusk-shreds,
>
> And bit by bit infringe
> A pond of dusty light,
> Spectral in shadow until they bobbingly one
> By one ignite.
>
> Neither pale nor bright,
> The turkey-cock parades
> Through radiant squalors, darkly auspicious as
> The ace of spades,

---

[11]Cummins, 35.

Himself his own cortége
And puffed with the pomp of death,
Rehearsing over and over with strangled râle
His latest breath.

The vast black body floats
Above the crossing knees
As a cloud over thrashed branches, a calm ship
Over choppy seas,

Shuddering its fan and feathers
In fine soft clashes
With the cold sound that the wind makes, fondling
Paper-ashes.

The pale-blue bony head
Sets on its shepherd's-crook
Like a saint's death-mask, turns a vague, superb
And timeless look

Upon these clocking hens
And the cocks that one by one,
Dawn after mortal dawn, with vulgar joy
Acclaim the sun.

Wilbur's gift for marvelous description creates a delightful barnyard scene which becomes the context for serious meditation on mortality. The turkey-cock is "darkly auspicious," "shuddering its fan and feathers," with a head "Like a saint's death-mask." "Himself his own cortége / And puffed with the pomp of death," the turkey knows it is November, when winter begins to set in and Americans enjoy his kind for Thanksgiving dinner. Perhaps it is the imminence of his death that lends dignity to his comic appearance and melodramatic behavior ("Rehearsing over and over with strangled râle / His latest breath"), or it may be our recognition that all life is as mysteriously supported as the precarious "vast black body" floating above unsteady and spindly legs. And surrounding the description of the "darkly auspicious" turkey there is a vibrant light imagery. "Nine white chickens . . . / . . . infringe / A pond of dusty light, / Spectral in shadow until they bobbingly one / By one ignite." The turkey looks "Upon these clocking hens / And the cocks that one by one / Dawn after mortal dawn, with vulgar joy / Acclaim the sun." The effect is that of putting the sunlight in conflict with death.[12] Indeed, Wilbur gives sunlight both the first and last word in this poem, so that the death of the pompous but endearing turkey is delicately balanced with daily joy.

"A Black November Turkey" is typical of Wilbur's work in that vivid descriptions are parlayed into religious and philosophical insights. What varies in such poems, however, is the degree to which Wilbur relies on his powers of observation in comparison to the degree he relies on his constructive imagination in coming to religiously significant insights. This does not indicate a shift in Wilbur's thinking over time or indecisiveness, but rather his sense that objective observation and the constructive imagination each have an appropriate role to play as one encounters the world.[13] Some of Wilbur's poems focus on the moment of observation. Some celebrate the mind's constructive role. Others attempt to capture the whole encounter.

Those poems written as if the mind were ultimately responsible for the shape of perception echo the poetry of Wallace Stevens.[14] For example, "The Beacon" (*TTW:NCP* 249-50) is strikingly reminiscent of Stevens' point of view and of his poem "Anecdote of the Jar." In Stevens' poem, an art object takes "dominion" of the landscape, providing a point of reference, an organizing principle, so that the wilderness is "no longer wild."[15] Similarly, in

---

[12]John P. Farrell, "The Beautiful Changes in Richard Wilbur's Poetry," in Salinger, 188.

[13]See Chapter One, 11-13.

[14]Stevens' high regard for the power of the creative imagination is well documented by Martz in the two final essays of *The Poem of the Mind*. Stevens is the poet of "the mind in the act of finding what will suffice." The mind is ultimately responsible for the shape of perception. Louis L. Martz, *The Poem of the Mind: Essays on Poetry/English and American* (London: Oxford University Press, 1969), 183-223.

[15]*The Collected Poems of Wallace Stevens* (New York: Alfred A. Knopf, 1978), 76.

"The Beacon" Wilbur spins out a conceit wherein the light from a lighthouse represents an active mind searching the chaos of reality. Reality is as deeply mysterious as the blackness of the sea at night with the sea representing perhaps both the inscrutability of the world outside the self and the unconscious depths within. The imagination (light), however, "with cutlass gaze" cuts through "the Gordian waters." "The beacon-blaze unsheathing turns / The face of darkness pale" and finally, like Stevens' jar, "a sighted ship / Assembles all the sea."

In "My Father Paints the Summer" (*BC:NCP* 363), it is evident that Wilbur's commitment to the constructive imagination derives in part from his admiration of his own father's art. He remembers in the poem a summer holiday during his childhood and how, when others became bored with conversation and ping pong in the resort hotel during a rainy spell, his father would leave them in the lobby. Then

> . . . up in his room by artificial light
> My father paints the summer, and his brush
> Tricks into sight
> The prosperous sleep, the girdling stir and clear steep hush
> Of a summer never seen,
> A granted green.

In the poem's final lines, Wilbur celebrates his father's ability to create a reality that transcends what is available to those less imaginative.

> There must be prime
> In the heart to beget that season, to reach past rain and find
> Riding the palest days
> Its perfect blaze.

"The Beacon" and "My Father Paints the Summer" celebrate the constructive imagination generally. "Digging for China" (*TTW:NCP* 256) delineates a specific role which Wilbur deems appropriate for the constructive imagination in the cultivation of religious insight.

"Far enough down is China," somebody said.
"Dig deep enough and you might see the sky
As clear as at the bottom of a well.
Except it would be real-a different sky.
Then you could burrow down until you came
To China! Oh, it's nothing like New Jersey.
There's people, trees, and houses, and all that,
But much, much different. Nothing looks the same."

I went and got the trowel out of the shed
And sweated like a coolie all that morning,
Digging a hole beside the lilac-bush,
Down on my hands and knees. It was a sort
Of praying, I suspect. I watched my hand
Dig deep and darker, and I tried and tried
To dream a place where nothing was the same.
The trowel never did break through to blue.

Before the dream could weary of itself
My eyes were tired of looking into darkness,
My sunbaked head of hanging down a hole.
I stood up in a place I had forgotten,
Blinking and staggering while the earth went round
And showed me silver barns, the fields dozing
In palls of brightness, patens growing and gone
In the tides of leaves, and the whole sky china blue.
Until I got my balance back again
All that I saw was China, China, China.

The boy's quest for China has much in common with religious questing. Christianity promises its converts that the familiar will seem different once they have "eyes to see." The boy wants to reach China because it promises a new way of seeing familiar "people, trees, and houses, and all that." Moreover, just as religious seekers prepare for their visions, the boy prepares for his. After trying to imagine China (stanza one), he got

"down on . . . hands and knees. It was a sort / Of praying, I suspect." And
though he "tried and tried / To dream a place where nothing was the same,"
he never got the dream just right and by his own effort he "never did break
through to blue." When the vision finally came, it came gratuitously after he
had given up on his own ability to reach his goal. Yet, one leaves this poem
knowing that he would never have had his vision of China unless he had
imagined something different than New Jersey and then devoted himself to
"looking into darkness." In a discussion of the "common features in the
creativity of scientist, artist, and mystic," Amos Wilder observes:

> I would suppose that neither Einstein's clarifying formula nor Dante's
> vision of the rose in the *Paradiso* were presented to them on a silver
> platter while they idled. No doubt meditation and a wise passivity and
> negative capability were involved, but also years of intense application. If
> this law holds for the genius it also holds for the rest of us. . . . Prior
> disciplines are the condition of significant vision.[16]

Wilder's conclusion is manifestly a part of Wilbur's understanding for
just as the boy's prior discipline is the condition of his vision, other seekers in
Wilbur's verse also obtain visions through discipline: from Bruno Sandoval
in "A Plain Song for Comadre" (*TTW:NCP* 244), to the insomniac "Walking
to Sleep" (*WS:NCP* 158-61), to the poet's own daughter in "The Writer"
(*MR:NCP* 53-4). These narrative characters reveal a pattern that extends to
Wilbur's lyrical poems as well. There too, disciplined observation and
painstaking craftsmanship engender intuitions of the spirit.

Nevertheless, it is true that Wilbur assigns the constructive
imagination an even more active role *after* perception than before. Memory
and deliberation grant an experience its richest and fullest interpretation.
Among the poems that make this point, "A Fire-Truck" (*AP:NCP* 207) is
especially vivid.

> Right down the shocked street with a siren-blast
> That sends all else skittering to the curb,
> Redness, brass, ladders and hats hurl past,
>   Blurring to sheer verb,

---

[16]Amos Niven Wilder, *Theopoetic: Theology and the Religious Imagination*
(Philadelphia: Fortress Press, 1976), 62-64.

Shift at the corner into uproarious gear
And make it around the turn in a squall of traction,
The headlong bell maintaining sure and clear,
    Thought is degraded action!

Beautiful, heavy, unweary, loud, obvious thing!
I stand here purged of nuance, my mind a blank.
All I was brooding upon has taken wing,
    And I have you to thank.

As you howl beyond hearing I carry you into my mind,
Ladders and brass and all, there to admire
Your phoenix-red simplicity, enshrined
    In that not extinguished fire.

The entrance of the fire-truck is so commanding that it is not until line three of stanza three that the speaker is able to describe the setting into which the fire-truck comes. Then the reader learns that the speaker was brooding about something, cerebrally preoccupied and less than alert to his environment. But the "Beautiful, heavy, unweary, loud, obvious thing" blasts into his awareness. "Blurring to sheer verb," it is pure vitality bearing the anti-intellectual message that "*thought is degraded action!*" The speaker is stunned into admiration: "purged of nuance, my mind a blank. / All I was brooding upon" gone. He is grateful to be cleansed and made part of a world where action prevails.

However, Wilbur is not content to end the poem after stanza two when the action in the street has been described, nor even at the end of stanza three when the immediate effect of the action on his mind has been reported. Stanza four celebrates the powers of memory and imagination. His memory enables the speaker to "admire" the fire-truck even after it has disappeared. His imagination creates a picture which captures the fire-truck's enduring beauty and significance: "phoenix-red simplicity, enshrined / In that not extinguished fire." "A Fire-Truck" does not argue for the superiority of either factual or imagined reality, but rather gives each its due. The mind cannot compete with fact in terms of commanding immediacy. But without the mind, "sheer verbs" have no chance to register their significance.

That the fire-truck has the capacity temporarily to take over the speaker's mind indicates that the constructive imagination must do its work within limits imposed by the tangible world. But Wilbur recognizes the imagination's tendency to forget its own limits. Several of his poems turn on the dramatic confrontation that comes when an overly ambitious imagination meets its match in a stubborn world. In "La Rose des Vents" (*C:NCP* 287), the imagination and world are personified in a poet and his lady. The poet wants to live in his dreams, but is opposed by his lady who says: "Forsake those roses / Of the mind / And tend the true, / The mortal flower." Neither speaker wins a clear rhetorical victory. So, too, in "The Aspen and the Stream" (*AP:NCP* 205-6), and "Poplar, Sycamore" (*BC:NCP* 381), where both points of view are rendered as attractive, and the reader is left to ponder (with Wilbur) how they may be reconciled. The mind's limitations are even more pointedly marked in "The Juggler" (*C:NCP* 297) and in "L'Etoile" (*C:NCP* 373). These poems suggest that there is a cost exacted of the human spirit when the realities of this world are forgotten.

In "An Event" (*TTW:NCP* 274), "words" are regarded as poetical constructs which sometimes give definition to this world and which sometimes are defeated by the world's reality which won't yield itself to definition. However, here the *conflict* between words and the world produces a more profound glimpse into the world's meaning than that offered by either words or the world alone:

> It is by words and the defeat of words,
> Down sudden vistas of the vain attempt,
> That for a flying moment one may see
> By what cross-purposes the world is dreamt.

This is what happens when the givens of tangible reality are rightly observed and the constructive imagination plays its proper role: a transcendental perspective emerges and one may see the world's purpose. The transcendental perspective in this poem is all the more powerfully presented by a series of puns. For, in Christianity, it is by the Word (Jesus Christ) and by the Word's defeat (at the crucifixion) that one may glimpse the world's purpose which is to provide a context for self-sacrificial love. The world's purposes are "cross-purposes."

Likewise, in "Mind" (*TTW:NCP* 240), it is not willful determination that accomplishes the mind's most impressive work, but rather "luck" coinciding with "error." That Wilbur describes the error as "graceful" indicates both its felicitousness and that it arrives as an unbidden, benevolent gift from outside oneself.

Thus, Wilbur's spiritual intuitions are of a reality that transcends the mind and is located within the tangible world. None of Wilbur's poems state this more directly than "The Eye" (*MR:NCP* 56-7). According to "The Eye," the poet must not only resist the Stevensian tendency to rely totally on the mind for the "supreme fiction," but must also resist all other attempts to find spiritual truths in abstractions. The protagonist of the poem is vacationing in St. Thomas and tells of spending an hour looking through his host's binoculars:

> What kept me goggling all that hour? The nice
> Discernment of a lime or lemon slice?
> A hope of lewd espials? An astounded
> Sense of the import of a thing surrounded-
> Of what a Z or almond-leaf became
> Within the sudden premise of a frame?
> All these, and that my eye should flutter there,
> By shrewd promotion, in the outstretched air,
> An unseen genius of the middle distance,
> Giddy with godhead or with nonexistence.

He recognizes that his aspirations have been misdirected. He confesses that his eye (also, the "I," first person singular) has left behind the visible world and thus lost contact with all reality: "there / . . . in the outstretched air . . . / Giddy with godhead or with nonexistence."

Part II begins "Preserve us, Lucy, / From the eye's nonsense"[17] and later continues, "Remind me that I am here in body, / A passenger, and

---

[17]Lucy is St. Lucy to whom this poem/prayer is addressed. She is the patroness of eyesight and served as Dante's guide in Canto II of *The Inferno*.

rumpled. / Charge me to see / in all bodies the beat of spirit." The poem ends,

> Let me be touched
> By the alien hands of love forever,
> That this eye not be folly's loophole
> But giver of due regard.

Pure art, purely mental constructs, are not the path to spiritual truth according to Wilbur; the most valuable, "rarest things are visible and firm" ("Lament" *C:NCP* 324). If one rejects the world in order to dwell in "a fabulous town / Immaculate, high, and never formed before . . . / The town of [the] mind's exacted vision," at first it will seem wonderful. But it will turn out to be "the mind's worst vanity" ("Clearness" *C:NCP* 313). Wilbur's message, over and over again, is that "It is the province of poems to make some order in the world, but poets can't afford to forget that there is a reality of things which survives all orders great and small. Things *are*. The cow is there. No poetry can have any strength unless it continually bashes itself against the reality of things" (*R* 217). It is by giving due regard to "all bodies" that we may see "the beat of spirit."

In Wilbur's epistemology, then, the world is observed with reverent attention because it is the locus of the spirit, and the constructive imagination most appropriately precedes the sacrosanct moment of perception with mental preparation and follows it with active reflection that leads to careful writing. The whole encounter involves the poet in a sort of dialogue with his environment. Wilbur is saying as much, I believe, when he recommends to contemporary poets an attitude of "devoutness" toward the world, a devoutness in which "neither the mysterious world nor the formative mind can be denied" (*R* 218-219).

In "Advice to a Prophet" (*AP:NCP* 182-3), Wilbur suggests that the most potent argument against nuclear weapons is that their use would put an end to this dialogue between persons and the world. Of more concern to us than the prospect of physical loss is the prospect of losing meaning from the lives of individuals and from the whole human family:

When you come, as you soon must, to the streets of our city,
Mad-eyed from stating the obvious,
Not proclaiming our fall but begging us
In God's name to have self-pity,

Spare us all word of the weapons, their force and range,
The long numbers that rocket the mind;
Our slow unreckoning hearts will be left behind,
Unable to fear what is too strange.

Nor shall you scare us with talk of the death of the race,
How should we dream of this place without us?–
The sun mere fire, the leaves untroubled about us,
A stone look on the stone's face?

Speak of the world's own change. Though we cannot conceive
Of an undreamt thing, we know to our cost
How the dreamt cloud crumbles, the vines are blackened by frost,
How the view alters. We could believe,

If you told us so, that the white tailed deer will slip
Into perfect shade, grown perfectly shy,
The lark avoid the reaches of our eye,
The jack-pine lose its knuckled grip

On the cold ledge, and every torrent burn
As Xanthus once, its gliding trout
Stunned in a twinkling. What should we be without
The dolphin's arc, the dove's return,

These things in which we have seen ourselves and spoken?
Ask us, prophet, how we shall call
Our natures forth when that live tongue is all
Dispelled, that glass obscured or broken

In which we have said the rose of our love and the clean
Horse of our courage, in which beheld
The singing locust of the soul unshelled,
And all we mean or wish to mean.

Ask us, ask us whether with the worldless rose
Our hearts shall fail us; come demanding
Whether there shall be lofty or long standing
When the bronze annals of the oak-tree close.

The prophet wants to tell what is obvious, that nuclear war would destroy the planet; and Wilbur urges that he shock us into an awareness of the enormity of our potential loss. But, he says, the rhetoric of "weapons, their force and range, / The long numbers that rocket the mind" will not convince "Our slow unreckoning hearts." Neither will "talk of the death of the race," for it too is beyond comprehension. So Wilbur proposes that the prophet "speak of the world's own change," to speak of familiar incidents of loss within the natural realm. Though the heart is "slow and unreckoning," it knows how to grieve. The human heart will know the pang of loss that comes when a familiar shape disappears in the clouds or when leaves change from vital green to deathly black due to an overnight frost. The losses from nuclear annihilation are these losses that we know so well made "perfect," total and final. Then the poet tells the prophet why the prospect of these losses touches us so deeply. He says just as the natural world cannot be itself without our projections of meaning; so, too, we ourselves are inexplicable without a world to provide apt metaphors for "all we mean and wish to mean." We are *homo loquens* and our language, the essence of our being, depends on the "live tongue" of nature. The prophet must remind us, in other words, that the self and nature are radically interdependent.[18]

---

[18]The late theologian Joseph Sittler quoted from "Advice to a Prophet" in an essay arguing that the grace of God is incarnational. He wrote that a renewal of theological and religious language concerning grace must rely on the assumption that "nature and grace, perception, experience, and wonder, the creation as the habitat of our bodies, and the divine redemption as the Word of God to our spirits, must all be held together in thought as indeed they occur together in fact." In a paragraph that could nearly stand as a paraphrase of the closing stanzas of "Advice to a Prophet," Sittler asks:

In an address broadcast by the Voice of America,[19] Wilbur contrasts two possible relationships between poets and the communities in which they dwell: he says that they can be "poet-citizens" or "alienated artists." Conscious that there are risks to each choice, Wilbur affirms his own preference for the role of the poet-citizen who undertakes to perform "a certain critical and expressive office . . . in the community" (*R* 115-116). And he appears to be enacting such a role in a poem like "Advice to a Prophet," where he takes up the position of counsel to those who would motivate the community to preserve itself. He writes as one who has something of value to offer his fellow citizens. And so he has, for he has cultivated intuitions of the spirit and found them life-sustaining in the face of this world's unspeakable evils. His articulation of what he has seen and his clarity about how he has come to his visions are offered to the public in his poems. They stand where others may make use of them in their own spiritual questing. Wilbur is equally intentional about his role as poet-citizen in other poems, especially "Still, Citizen Sparrow" (*C:NCP* 318), "Castles and Distances" (*C:NCP* 289-91), "Next Door" (*AP:NCP* 223-4), "A Simplification" (*BC:NCP* 371), "After the Last Bulletins" (*TTW:NCP* 241-2), and "The Fourth of July" (*MR:NCP* 69-70).

Wilbur has, of course, his own particular way of enacting this role, and other poets perform it differently. Denise Levertov and Robert Bly, for example, became spokespersons for the anti-war movement during the Vietnam era. Indeed, so identified did they become with that cause that for several years it furnished the principal inspiration for their poetry. Wilbur's

---

Does it mean nothing for our reality as persons that the natural world which is not human is yet to the human a life-sustaining placenta of self-consciousness? Is it without force that metaphors drawn from that world have been immemorially necessary when men have sought to find a language ample enough and powerful enough to celebrate or lament the "glories of our blood and state?"

Without using theological language as Sittler does, Wilbur's poem also advocates the interdependence of self and nature as necessary for authentic spiritual insight. Joseph Sittler, "Grace and a Sense For the World," in *Essays on Nature and Grace* (Philadelphia: Fortress Press, 1972), 93-94, 108.

[19]Published as part of *Poets on Poetry* in 1966, and found in *R* 115-126.

work during the same period was probing the ways in which our nation's deeper structures of consciousness are shaped by violence and impersonality. Therefore, he was no less engaged with the central public drama of the time than "activist" poets. Yet his disinclination to commit his poetry to the advocacy of particular programs or policies has led some to charge him with neutrality and indifference–simply because his way of approaching the public realm differs from that of poets such as Levertov or Bly. This has in turn prompted in Wilbur a certain intransigence. As Bruce Michelson says in his review of *The Mind-Reader*:

> The poems are as witty and elegant and deadly serious as ever, but the collection, taken altogether, seems to stand up against every kind of poet-chic, as if Wilbur meant to strut around for a moment, with an angry glint in his eye, wearing the "bourgeois" mask which his detractors hang on him. The defiance runs cover to cover, literally; the jacket front shows a silhouette of somebody sitting with legs crossed at a cafe table, evidently recollecting in too much tranquility; the back is a photograph of The Poet in the Parlor, looking tweedy and comfy and sane–looking all wrong.[20]

Wilbur's defiance of those who would tell him how he *should* fulfill his role as poet-citizen is taken by Michelson to have become a part of his basic stance in the collection of his poems that he issued in 1976 in *The Mind-Reader*, but it is actually noticeable in his collection of 1969, *Walking to Sleep*.[21] A case in point is "A Late Aubade" (*WS:NCP* 153), originally published in *The New Yorker* in 1968. While the Vietnam War raged, while ghettoes exploded in riots, and assassinations stained American public life, he dared to publish a poem whose quiet urbanity discusses none of these things:[22]

---

[20]Bruce Michelson, "Richard Wilbur's *The Mind-Reader*" in Salinger, 132.

[21]See also Wilbur's comments in "The Bottles Become New, Too" (*R* 215-223), and in *Twentieth Century Authors, First Supplement* (see chap. 1, note 13), both from much earlier in his career.

[22]In addition, in spite of this poem's loving and tender tone, feminists will question the sensitivity of a poet who writes in this way about women's interests and "a woman's reckoning." A later poem, "The Catch" (*NCP* 17-18), also clearly domestic in origin, is similarly loving and tender, but also a document of unreconstructed chauvinism. Wilbur's traditionalism in poetics, social attitudes, and politics, is irritating to those of a more

You could be sitting now in a carrel
Turning some liver-spotted page,
Or rising in an elevator-cage
Toward Ladies' Apparel.

You could be planting a raucous bed
Of salvia, in rubber gloves,
Or lunching through a screed of someone's loves
With pitying head,

Or making some unhappy setter
Heel, or listening to a bleak
Lecture on Schoenberg's serial technique.
Isn't this better?

Think of all the time you are not
Wasting, and would not care to waste,
Such things, thank God, not being to your taste.
Think what a lot

---

progressive bent, yet Bruce Michelson (in a later reflection) is persuasive as he applauds Wilbur for including domesticity as an aspect of life worthy of poetic attention. His comments on "A Late Aubade" are particularly helpful; "this is self-evidently love-talk between people who do not have to strike political poses for each other in bed." He goes on to suggest that Wilbur is very much aware that this song is "late," expressing attitudes that belong to an earlier era. The tone is light and self-deprecating, having fun at the expense of its own chauvinism, for "the poem has come along late in the aged and possibly exhausted tradition of occasional love verse." See Bruce Michelson, *Wilbur's Poetry: Music in a Scattering Time* (Amherst: The University of Massachusetts Press, 1991), 9-12. Indeed, Wilbur's poetry consistently begins with the world and the poet's sensibilities wherever they are, flaws readily exposed, from the poet's failures to keep in step with his times to the evidence that social structures and nature itself are infected by radical evil. Nevertheless, Wilbur's poems (as this and subsequent chapters reveal) locate this quotidian world in the context of transcendent mysteries which address our alienations and give our lives profound definition

> Of time, by woman's reckoning,
> You've saved, and so may spend on this,
> You who had rather lie in bed and kiss
> Than anything.
>
> It's almost noon, you say? If so,
> Time flies, and I need not rehearse
> The rosebuds-theme of centuries of verse.
> If you *must* go,
>
> Wait for a while, then slip downstairs
> And bring us up some chilled white wine,
> And some blue cheese, and crackers, and some fine
> Ruddy-skinned pears.

· Perhaps Wilbur had such a poem as this in mind when he suggested in a letter to George Abbot White written on the last day of December, 1967, that it was the poet's task to keep alive what the protestors would want to "come home to." The letter struggles interestingly with the relationship of his poetry to world affairs:

Dear Mr. White,

What a tough question you propose. Yeats once found it easy, or found that it made a good poem, to say that the poet should chuck world affairs and concentrate on addressing the hearts of old men or young girls. Yet he did, after all, have to write about politics and the drift of his violent times. The poems were mostly good, I expect, because (regardless of the validity or invalidity of his cyclical theory) he took a complex and tragic view rather than a simplified partisan stance. I just came across this poem by John Peale Bishop:

> Harder it is to sing than shout
> And rotten, rotten is the age.
> But what are all these poets about,
> Their throats constricted by their rage?

That seems to me correct–that rage makes for bad poetry. I suppose that if one cannot be other than directly and absolutely furious, if the sensibility narrows into political urgency, then one should turn to action rather than write a poetry which sacrifices the right to mixed feelings and reservations, and so debases itself. The action might take the form, as it did for Milton, of some other kind of writing, a pamphleteering kind. This Viet Nam war being as detestable as it is, I could respect anyone who made that choice–as I respected Dashiell Hammett, a veteran of the first World War, for volunteering to be a common soldier in the second. On the other hand, the poet is a specialist in the articulation of our present and timeless plights, and an emergency fabricator of comprehensive mental balances, and it may be that our need of him is greatest at such times as this, when most men's minds are turning into blunt instruments. Do you remember Karl Shapiro's poem about the conscientious objector, which said that the objector's conscience is what the soldiers come home to? Something analogous might be argued about the poet, in relation to the protestors, and to all others who have simplified themselves through contention. Finally, I guess that it is a matter of timing, of how bad things have become; if we have come to Salamis, than Aeschylus' right arm is worth more than his pen. For myself, I don't think we are quite there yet.

Anyway, thank you for what you say about "On The Marginal Way," and your report of Don Hall's reading it to his class in Michigan. I wish you well with the critical biography of Matty.[23]

I would like sometime to talk with you about him, although I think that I was always rather obtuse in my relations with him.

With good wishes,
Richard Wilbur

This letter does indeed constitute an important document for the student of Wilbur's poetry, for it clearly indicates that he is one by no means disengaged from social and political actuality, and it reminds us that, when he does turn to politics, he strives for "a complex and tragic view rather than a simplified partisan stance."

"The Fourth of July" (*MR:NCP* 69-70), which in 1977 Anthony Hecht predicted would "be the best thing to come out of the American Bicentennial,"[24] is probably Wilbur's most impressive effort as poet-citizen. In it, he assumes the "peculiar imaginative burden" that he sees belonging to

---

[23]At the time of his correspondence with Wilbur, George Abbott White was working on a critical biography of F.O. Matthiessen.

[24]Hecht, in Salinger, 130.

American poet-citizens by virtue of "the incoherence of America" (*R* 116). It is also an appropriate poem with which to end this chapter, because it recapitulates in a political context many of the issues this chapter has already considered in a religious context. For example, the coexistence of evil and a benevolent transcendence prompted Wilbur's insight that encounters with evil may toughen the human spirit and enable "starker sight." "The Fourth of July" ponders the coexistence of human evil and political ideals, and moves toward an overarching notion that might as well hold them together in creative tension. And, just as Wilbur's religious questing settled into an effort to develop a language about his spiritual intuitions which would have integrity, so, too, "The Fourth of July" looks finally to the integrity of language as vital for our political future.

Parts one and two of "The Fourth of July" offer contrasting scenes that, Wilbur informs us in a note, both took place on July 4, 1862. On that date, Charles Dodgson, who wrote under the pseudonym of Lewis Carroll, invented his marvelous stories of Alice in Wonderland, and Ulysses S. Grant plotted his seige of Vicksburg.

1.

Liddell, the Oxford lexicographer
Allowed his three small daughters on this day
To row from Folly Bridge to Godstow, where
Their oarsman, Mr. Dodgson, gave them tea
Beneath a rick of hay,
Shading their minds with golden fantasy.
And it was all fool's gold,
Croquet or caucus madder than a hare,
That universe of which he sipped and told,
Mocking all grammars, codes, and theorems
Beside the spangled, blindly flowing Thames.

2.

Off to the west, in Memphis, where the sun's
Mid-morning fire beat on a wider stream,
His purpose headstrong as a river runs,
Grant closed a smoky door on aides and guards

And chewed through scheme on scheme
For toppling Vicksburg like a house of cards.
The haze at last would clear
On Hard Times Landing, Porter's wallowed guns,
The circling trenches that in just a year
Brought the starved rebels through the settling smoke
To ask for terms beside a stunted oak.

Together these stanzas remind us that at all times delight coexists with harsh reality. An honest appraisal of our country's past on the Fourth of July in America's bicentennial year would have had to reckon with both realities. Even though part three goes on to ask how to integrate conceptually America's checkered past, and the rest of the poem provides an answer, one possible relationship already is alluded to in part one. The allusions are to Lewis Carroll, specifically to the poems which precede *Alice's Adventures in Wonderland* and *Through the Looking Glass: And What Alice Found There*. In the first, three children beg for a nonsensical story to relieve their wearisome rowing. The poem says that the author's response is "the tale of Wonderland" and, once told, "home we steer, a merry crew, / Beneath the setting sun." The other poem suggests that the children's pleasure and relief are possible for adults, too, for "We are but older children, dear, / Who fret to find our bedtime near." Words, especially words of fantasy, are real enough to protect one from some of the harshness of life: "The magic words shall hold the fast: / Thou shalt not heed the raving blast."[25] Perhaps Wilbur is suggesting that in America's difficult times, we also may shade our minds with "golden fantasy," finding respite and refreshment there. By the end of "The Fourth of July," however, this suggestion will seem inadequate.

Against the contrasting scenes in parts one and two and the diverse realities for which they stand, in part three Wilbur raises the very question he is most equipped to ask as poet-citizen: how does one make sense of what one sees? He asks if there is a "grand arcanum" (any possible verbal adequacy) to hold together Dodgson and Grant in the coincidental but

---

[25]Lewis Carroll, *Alice's Adventures in Wonderland* and *Through the Looking Glass: And What Alice Found There* (New York: Random House, 1946).

disparate scenes of parts one and two. Is there some word that "holds all from foundering in points and waves"? This third stanza concludes without suggesting any new and comprehensive word. But it does suggest that even though they may not have a proper name for the phenomenon, Americans have believed that mysteriously all things do hold together. To make this suggestion, Wilbur once again alludes to Lewis Carroll: specifically to Alice's adventures in the "termless wood." There Alice meets a fawn but cannot tell it her name or find a name for it. As long as Alice and the fawn are without names, "they walk on together through the wood, Alice with her arms clasped lovingly round the soft neck of the fawn." Once out of the woods, however, the fawn and Alice discover who they are, and the fawn "darts away at full speed."[26] In "The Fourth of July" Wilbur muses,

> No doubt the fairest game
> Play only in those groves where creatures are
> At one, distinct, and innocent of name,
> As Alice found, who in the termless wood
> Lacked words to thank the shade in which she stood.

Alice's friendship with the fawn gave her temporary security in that strange and often frightening Wonderland. Even so, the shade of the unnamed tree gave her temporary shelter from the sun. I think Wilbur is implying that vague assertions of America's unity and chauvinistic affirmations of America's glorious past are like Alice's brief visit to the "termless wood." Jingoism offers no adequate vocabulary, no words to hold together all that is America. Eventually we will have to face the divisions within our nation and the unpleasant realities of our history as certainly as Alice and the fawn had to face their incompatibility.

In the poem's final two stanzas, Wilbur turns to Linnaeus and Copernicus as resources for the renewal of language about America. Their approach to the world around them is exemplary for a people unable to name its nation's heritage and character. Wilbur turns for help to scientists who were open to the world, unfettered by existing conceptual systems, and ready to organize the diverse data confronting them.

---

[26]Lewis Carroll, *Through the Looking Glass*, 41- 50.

Part four is about Linnaeus, the great eighteenth century Swedish botanist. Wilbur informs us that "Owing to a stroke, Linnaeus lost 'the knowledge even of his own name'" (*MR:NCP* 112). In contrast to the story of Alice which depicts her loss of verbal adequacy as a charming exaggeration of essential innocence, the innocence of a stroke victim is not charming at all. It underscores the cost of innocence no matter what has caused it. Linnaeus may stand, then, both as a symbol of America's forgetfulness of its past and of its hope for future articulation of the national ethos.

4.

Nevertheless, no kindly swoon befell
Tree-named Linnaeus[27]
when the bald unknown
Encroached upon his memory, cell by cell,
And he, whose love of all things made had brought
Bird, beast, fish, plant, and stone
Into the reaches of his branchy thought,
Lost bitterly to mind
Their names' sweet Latin and his own as well.
Praise to all fire-fledged knowledge of the kind
That, stooped beneath a hospital roof,
Brings only hunch and gaiety for proof,

Linnaeus, the quintessential namer, had brought "all things made" into "his branchy thought" out of love. His love, formed in the process of gaining knowledge of the beloved, was of a different type than Alice's for the fawn in the termless wood. Hers had more in common with an infant's sense of oneness with an undifferentiated environment. His was love born of mature wonder at the world around him, and the loss of his love brings bitterness rather than naiveté. And yet Wilbur offers a paean to that "fire-fledged" knowledge which has been robbed of its extensiveness and confined, "stooped beneath a hospital roof." Even stunted, that truth brings "hunch and gaiety." Forgotten words strain toward rediscovery. In the fifth and final part

---

[27]Wilbur's notes report that Linnaeus's family took their name from a tall Linden tree near their home (*MR:NCP* 111-12).

of "The Fourth of July," Wilbur praises Copernicus whose knowledge was not confined but rather expansive and visionary:

> His vision leapt into the solar disc
> And set the earth to wheeling,

Also, Copernicus was "Not hesitant to risk / His dream-stuff in the fitting rooms of fact." Copernicus's "golden fantasy" has among its virtues that it has been corroborated (and adjusted to conform) with the facts. Wilbur ends his poem by also praising "these states" for their ability to adjust the meaning of their words "in the fitting-rooms of fact." It has been a long and painful process, he says, but finally America has begun to understand the language of the Declaration of Independence in a new way. America has come to see that "black men too are men," and so the rights and aspirations claimed by the Declaration are to be extended to all America's citizens.

Therein is Wilbur's solution to America's identity crisis. Instead of retreating into fantasy, denial, or vagueness, Wilbur urges his fellow citizens to claim all their national heritage–the grand and the shameful. He urges them to incorporate the past into an idea of America as a nation that has struggled toward the truth, a nation that has grown toward its identity. To articulate that identity, the poem implies, one may remember the words of the Declaration of Independence, first read on the Fourth of July. But one must understand that for America to be true to herself today, those words must shape the political and social milieu of *all* this nation's people.

Typically, Wilbur has gathered the several issues raised in "The Fourth of July" under the umbrella issue of the integrity of language: the states are praised for "beginning . . . / To mean what once we said upon this day." His proposal in the political realm resembles that which he has made in the spiritual realm. As this chapter set out to demonstrate, in the spiritual realm Wilbur explores forces inimical to spirituality and concludes that they may toughen the human spirit, giving "starker sight." With starker sight, Wilbur prepares himself to receive what the world has to offer, and then curbs any inclination of the imagination to distort vision. He keeps the moment of perception sacrosanct. Then he probes what he has seen for truth and implication with the considerable reflective power at his command. Finally, he crafts his works with skill and offers them to the community. His carefully worded spiritual insights have integrity because they have been tested by evil, tested by openness, tested by analytical reflection, and tested by the community.

"The Fourth of July" is the result of the same process. Wilbur's poem offers a "tragic and complex" interpretation of the American Bicentennial. His political suggestion to the nation has survived the same testing as his spiritual insights. Whether Wilbur concerns himself directly with intuitions of the spirit in an imperfect world or is led into the political arena by concerns he shares with his fellow citizens, he is indeed a "specialist in the articulation of our present and timeless plights, and an emergency fabricator of comprehensive mental balances."[28]

---

[28]From Wilbur's letter to George Abbott White. See above, p. 49.

Chapter Three

WILBUR AS MEDITATIVE POET

A meditative poem records . . . a self that is, ideally, one with itself, with other human beings, with created nature, and with the supernatural. . . . The self created in this poetry is . . . one that feels the hand of the supernatural upon himself and upon all created things. . . . On the other hand, it is true that the term "meditation" designates a process of the mind, rather than a particular subject matter: a full definition of the meditative poem, it seems, should be broad enough to include certain poems that are not concerned with the religious or the supernatural, in our usual sense of those words.

Louis Martz

Richard Wilbur's intuitions of the spirit are recorded in forms that enable his readers to retrace the poet's paths to spiritual discovery. His poems, most characteristically, start with an encounter within this world and move toward a realization that this world is surrounded by and interfused with another which is mysterious and wondrous. In this way Wilbur resembles poets writing in the genre Louis Martz denominated as "meditative poetry." Moreover, meditative poetry addresses issues of interest to Wilbur (as shown in Chapter Two): the role of the intellect in art, the function of art in life, and the relation of the self to others, nature, and the supernatural. In addition, as this chapter will show, some of the poetic forms and technical practices which Martz associated with meditative poetry are frequently found in Wilbur's poems. In Chapter Four I will discuss ways in which Wilbur's range of poetic strategies and perceptions of ecstatic experience expand Martz's genre.

The poetic structure Martz first discovered in English Metaphysical Poetry and which led to his postulation of a new genre is derived from formal religious meditation. Martz saw that poems by Southwell, Donne, Herbert, and Crashaw were similar in structure to the formulae for meditation found in several spiritual exercises developed during the Counter Reformation.[1] Martz summarizes the pattern most succinctly in his book *The Poem of the Mind*:

> It begins with the deliberate creation of a setting and the placing there of an actor, some aspect of the self; this is the famous composition of place recommended by the Jesuit exercises. This is followed by predominantly intellectual analysis of some crucial problem pertaining to that self; and it all ends in a highly emotional resolution where the projected self and the whole mind of the meditator come together in a spirit of devotion. This threefold process is related to the old division of the soul into memory, understanding, and will; the exercise of meditation integrates these faculties.[2]

Martz's essays suggest that later poets, such as Hopkins and Eliot, have also practiced formal meditation. Furthermore, as he claims, many other poets of a meditative bent who do not follow formal religious disciplines nevertheless end up writing poems resembling exemplars of the genre. I do not know whether or not Wilbur meditates according to any prescribed regimen, but "A Hole in the Floor" (*AP:NCP* 189-90) is one poem that certainly follows the pattern just described, and there are many others.

Stanzas one and two of "A Hole in the Floor" involve the "deliberate creation of a setting and the placing there of an actor, some aspect of the self."

> The carpenter's made a hole
> In the parlor floor, and I'm standing
> Staring down into it now

---

[1]Louis L. Martz, *The Poetry of Meditation: A Study in English Religious Literature of the Seventeenth Century*, rev. ed. (New Haven: Yale University Press, 1962), 5-6, 25-70.

[2]Louis L. Martz, *The Poem of the Mind: Essays on Poetry/English and American* (London: Oxford University Press, 1969), 215.

At four o'clock in the evening,
As Schliemann stood when his shovel
Knocked on the crowns of Troy.

A clean-cut sawdust sparkles
On the grey, shaggy laths,
And here is a cluster of shavings
From the time when the floor was laid,
They are silvery-gold, the color
Of Hesperian apple-parings.

Wilbur has rendered the setting at once precisely and evocatively. It is a particular room, the one with a hole in the floor; and it is a particular moment, four o'clock in the evening. The particularity of the room is further defined by use of the old-fashioned designation, "parlor." The "actor, some aspect of the self," is like the archaeological pioneer, Heinrich Schliemann, who also dug down to uncover a previously hidden record of the past. Schliemann's scientific quest was to prove that the Homeric legend of Troy was, in fact, historical. Schliemann's curiosity was fired by the power of myth and legend. The protagonist of the poem, like Schliemann, stands on the border between modern empiricism and openness to myth. In stanza two there is a similar juxtaposition of fact (the "sawdust" and "shavings") and mythological reference ("Hesperian apples"). Together they reinforce our sense of the speaker's location between the empirical and the mythical.

Stanzas three and four are the "analysis," an elaborate conceit:

Kneeling, I look in under
Where the joists go into hiding.
A pure street, faintly littered
With bits and strokes of light,
Enters the long darkness
Where its parallels will meet.

The radiator pipe
Rises in middle distance

Like a shuttered kiosk, standing
Where the only news is night.
Here it's not painted green,
As it is in the visible world.

The conceit is surrealistic and heightens the reader's awareness that the
empirically verifiable situation is accompanied by mystery and strangeness,
perhaps even terror.[3] There is a conflict being waged between opposite,
elemental, even sexual forces: a "pure" street is "faintly littered"; "bits and
strokes of light" invade "the long darkness." This strange world is not the
visible world. The kiosk (whose function it is to distribute information) is
shuttered: "the only news is night." The tone of Wilbur's conceit is not
"predominantly intellectual" as Martz would have it in his account of the
pattern of meditation in *The Poem of the Mind*. However, the tradition
behind Martz's schema includes ample precedent for the predominance of
emotions in these stanzas.[4] Disquiet pervades the speaker's understanding as
he gazes into the long darkness.

The final two stanzas contain an expression of "affections" and are
indeed a "resolution where the projected self and the whole mind of the
meditator come together in a spirit of devotion." "The climax, the aim and
end, of the whole exercise is achieved when the soul thus reformed is lifted
up to speak with God and to hear God speak to man in turn."[5] Wilbur's
penultimate stanza may be seen as the poet's address to God, his invocation

---

[3]"The poem is dedicated to René Magritte (1898-1967), French surrealist painter,
whose terrifying pictures of ordinary scenes are evoked in this poem." Richard Ellmann
and Robert O'Clair, eds., *The Norton Anthology of Modern Poetry* (New York: W.W.
Norton & Company, Inc., 1973), 1008 n.8.

[4]As Martz recognizes in a more extended explanation of the process, the Ignatian
exercises do not claim correspondence between the three steps (creation of a setting,
analysis, and colloquy) and the divisions of the soul (memory, understanding, and will).
Memory, understanding, and will may all be called upon for any of the steps. Martz,
Poetry of Meditation, 34-36. For an example within the Ignatian exercises, see David L.
Fleming, S.J., *The Spiritual Exercises of St. Ignatius: A Literal Translation and A
Contemporary Reading* (St. Louis: The Institute of Jesuit Sources, 1978), 34.

[5]Martz, *The Poetry of Meditation*, 36.

taking the casual form of a mild curse.[6] The final stanza is God's Word in
return, the "strange" revelation of light and love:

> For God's sake, what am I after?
> Some treasure, or tiny garden?
> Or that untrodden place,
> The house's very soul,
> Where time has stored our footbeats
> And the long skein of our voices?

> Not these, but the buried strangeness
> Which nourishes the known:
> That spring from which the floor-lamp
> Drinks now a wilder bloom,
> Inflaming the damask love-seat
> And the whole dangerous room.

What is the speaker after? "Treasure" could refer to cash hidden
beneath the floorboards, or it could stand for spiritual truth as it did in Jesus's
parable of the Hidden Treasure (Matthew 13:44). The "garden" could be a
pastoral respite from the urban scenes called up in the poem's middle section,
or it could be the original innocence of Eden. Getting to "the house's very
soul," where the past is all present, seems to be a way to gain control over the
past, either by means of recollection as in Freudian analysis or by assuming
the perspective of divine omniscience.[7]

"Not these," begins stanza six. Not these inherited images of the end
of our human quest, but the ground of their allure. This quest is for the
"buried strangeness," wherein that which is known rests and is nourished.[8]

---

[6]Similar ambiguities (is he really referring to God or just recording an expletive?)
are found in "Tywater" *BC:NCP* 342, and "Advice to a Prophet" *AP:NCP* 182-3.

[7]See Mircea Eliade, *Myth and Reality*, trans. Willard R. Trask (New York:
Harper and Row, 1963), 65, 86-89.

[8]Though this buried strangeness is never precisely described in Wilbur's work, he
intuits a mystical realm informed by Christian imagery. It has many of the qualities
Christianity attributes to the Kingdom of God, though Wilbur is careful to avoid any

The poem's central image for "buried strangeness" is light, and the meanings of light in Christian imagery contribute greatly to the power of the final stanza. The floor lamp spreads a supernatural light which is "wilder" than natural light, and the whole room becomes dangerous as the holy is dangerous.[9] Moreover, within the dangerous room, the damask love seat is "inflamed" by the light, as if a radical Christian passion had transformed the end of love from benevolence to martyrdom. These associations color the "resolution [of the poem] where the projected self and the whole mind of the meditator come together in a spirit of devotion." Here, integration occurs as the self moves from the border of the empirical and the mythical into the "buried strangeness," that is, into the mystical realm. In the mystical realm, the speaker's selfhood is most whole, united with the source of its vitality and identity. Thus, the structure and movement of this poem is precisely that of "meditative poetry."

Another element of meditative poetry which is frequently found in Wilbur's work is "interior dramatization." Martz defines interior dramatization as, "interaction between a projected, dramatized part of the self, and the whole mind of meditative man."[10] Sometimes Martz describes this interior drama in religious terms: "The speaker . . . talks to God within the self, . . . projects a self upon an inner stage, and there comes to know that self in the light of a divine presence."[11] On other occasions, this aspect of meditative poetry is described without recourse to religious terminology.[12] In either case, the self is understood to be a complex entity in the process of becoming more self-aware and struggling toward a sense of unity, or at least inward harmony. And several of Wilbur's poems exemplify Martz's concept of interior dramatization.

---

description which would narrow the referential range of his poems to a single dogmatic system.

[9]Rudolf Otto, *The Idea of the Holy*, trans. John W. Harvey (London: Oxford University Press, 1958), 12-24, 72-81.

[10]Martz, *The Poem of the Mind*, 7.

[11]Martz, *The Poem of the Mind*, 33.

[12]Martz, *The Poetry of Meditation*, 330.

One thinks most especially of those poems which contain two voices presenting divergent points of view, such as "La Rose des Vents" (*C:NCP* 287), "Two Voices in a Meadow" (*AP:NCP* 181), "The Aspen and the Stream" (*AP:NCP* 205-6), and "Epistemology" (*C:NCP* 288). And one also thinks of poems in which two or more points of view are explicitly weighed by the poem's protagonist, such as "Altitudes" (*TTW:NCP* 231), "Walking to Sleep" (*WS:NCP* 158-61), "Looking Into History" (*TTW:NCP* 252-3), and "A Baroque Wall-Fountain in the Villa Sciarra" (*TTW:NCP* 271-3). Regarding this last poem, Wilbur remarks, "What one hears in most of it is a single meditative voice balancing argument and counterargument, feeling and counterfeeling" (*R* 121).

In "A Baroque Wall-Fountain," Wilbur uses a meditative voice to muse about different understandings of human nature and to focus on the relationship of ecstasy and order. The first possibility entertained by the meditative self is expressed by the baroque fountain mentioned in the poem's title:

> Under the bronze crown
> Too big for the head of the stone cherub whose feet
>   A serpent has begun to eat,
> Sweet water brims a cockle and braids down
>
>   Past spattered mosses, breaks
> On the tipped edge of a second shell, and fills
>   The massive third below. It spills
> In threads then from the scalloped rim, and makes
>
>   A scrim or summery tent
> For a faun-ménage and their familiar goose.

Here the form is mimetically suited to the subject matter.[13] Long sentences open the poem and are "an effort to imitate the trickling down of

---

[13]The form is, I believe, Wilbur's invention: the stress and rhyme scheme being 3a5b4b5a. Wilbur uses the same form in "Altitudes." Hill, 99.

the water."[14] The rhymes mime the repetition of the fountain's shell motif. The rhythm repeatedly pauses for caesura and then tumbles forward in anapests or "drips" regularly in iambics.

In the midst of these descriptive lines, there are several hints that contrasting visions of self and world will be debated more explicitly later on. Wilbur notes that the bronze crown is "too big" for the cherub in the fountain. A representative of heaven (the cherub) is being eaten by a representative of hell (the serpent). The water is described as sweet, perhaps meaning it is tempting and dangerous. It is *falling*, after all, and may be headed for the realm of sin and lawlessness. And yet these are only connotations. The tone is predominantly that of delighted description. The reader's attention follows the water's descent and passes too quickly over the scene to be alarmed by these hints of trouble.

The lines that follow bring to the fore the question as to how to interpret the vision expressed by this fountain:

> Happy in all that ragged, loose
> Collapse of water, its effortless descent
>
> And flatteries of spray,
> The stocky god upholds the shell with ease,
>   Watching, about his shaggy knees,
> The goatish innocence of his babes at play;
>
> His fauness all the while
> Leans forward, slightly, into a clambering mesh
>   Of water-lights, her sparkling flesh
> In a saecular ecstasy, her blinded smile
>
> Bent on the sand floor
> Of the trefoil pool, where ripple-shadows come
>   And go in swift reticulum
> More addling to the eye than wine, and more

---

[14]Wilbur, quoted by Hill, 99.

> Interminable to thought
> Than pleasure's calculus. . . .

In these lines it is clear that the figures on the lower levels of the fountain are "happy," and more than happy– "in a saecular ecstasy." The scene is classically Dionysian: the water is in "ragged, loose / Collapse." The god has "shaggy knees," and his children are playing in "goatish innocence."[15] The drama is in the conflict between the prevailing tone and the increasingly explicit hints of dissatisfaction with this particular vision of human nature: is the "*saecular* ecstasy" of the sculpted scene satisfying or spiritually impoverished? On the one hand, the rhythm and sonic devices, including rhyme, communicate an apparently pleasurable vision. On the other hand, certain words, laden with connotations drawn from Christian Scripture and Greek mythology, question this facade of happiness. The *Oxford English Dictionary* reports, for example, that "goatish" is a figurative expression for a "licentious man" and can mean "lascivious" and "lustful." (How innocent can "goatish innocence" be?) The fauness has "sparkling flesh," and flesh in the Paulinian lexicon can refer to that in this world which has fallen away from faith in God. The ecstasy is reported to be "saecular," "Belonging to the world and its affairs as distinguished from the church and religion, . . . non-sacred."[16] The fauness has a "blinded smile," blind being a common Christian metaphor for a lack of spiritual enlightenment. In addition, she is "addled" by the moving pattern of light and shadow, more deeply affected than if she were merely drunk with wine or taken up in sensual pleasure.[17] In short, though the dominant tone of this passage is

---

[15]Sir James Frazer says: "As a goat [Dionysus] can hardly be separated from minor divinities, the Pans, Satyrs, and Silenuses, all of whom are closely associated with him and are represented more or less completely in the form of goats. Further, the fauns, the Italian counterpart of the Greek Pans and Satyrs, are described as being half goats, with goat feet and goat horns." *The New Golden Bough: A New Abridgement of the Classic Work by Sir James George Frazer*, ed. Theodor H. Gaster (New York: The New American Library, Inc., Mentor Books, 1964), 522.

[16]*Oxford English Dictionary*, s.v. "saecular."

pleasurable, Wilbur's imagery and vocabulary strongly suggest that this baroque fountain does indeed figure forth a profound disorder.

The next six lines provide the primary pivot for the poem, a transition from one possible vision of human nature to another:

> . . . Yet since this all
> Is pleasure, flash, and waterfall
> Must it not be too simple? Are we not
>
> More intricately expressed
> In the plain fountains that Maderna set
> Before St. Peter's–

Wilbur's word play is especially transparent here as he considers simplicity and intricacy. My reading has suggested that the baroque fountain is not simple at all. Furthermore, the questions as to how to take the sculptor's intentions and as to whether they truly represent human nature are anything but simple. And yet, if the fountain represents sensuality without spirituality, it truly distorts human nature by being simplistic. If the "plain" fountains to be described in the next ten lines include an exploration of the spiritual, then a more complete and complex understanding of human nature may emerge. Indeed,

> . . . Are we not
>
> More intricately expressed
> In the plain fountains that Maderna set
> Before St. Peter's–the main jet
> Struggling aloft until it seems at rest

---

[17]The play of light and shadow occurs in several poems by Wilbur. The way in which he uses that image in other poems strengthens the possibility that here it is meant to take the fauness to a deeper, more mysterious, and more threatening level of reality. Besides "Part of a Letter" (see Chapter One, pages 18-19), one could point to "Statues" (*TTW:NCP* 251). In that poem maple trees are blown by gusts of wind and go through "cloudy metamorphoses, / Their shadows all a brilliant disrepair" contributing to "a view / Lively as Ovid's Chaos, and its rich / Uncertainty."

In the very act of rising, until
The very wish of water is reversed,
That heaviness borne up to burst
In a clear, high, cavorting head, to fill

With blaze, and then in gauze
Delays, in a gnatlike shimmering, in a fine
Illumined version of itself, decline,
And patter on the stones its own applause?

Once again Wilbur's sentence structure mimetically represents the water's movement. Quickly the water is propelled to the top of its trajectory. Nearly as quickly it will fall, "decline, / And patter on the stones." In between it seems to hang in the air precariously struggling to defy gravity for several lines. The lines contain caesura interrupting the rhythm, each one causing the reader to ask: will the water fall back to earth now? . . . now? . . . now? Suspense is built until, at last, the decline begins.

Whereas the baroque fountain had Dionysian characteristics, this fountain has clean lines and bears the character of an intellectually satisfying work of art. No part of it is "too big" or "ragged" or "loose." In these ways it is Apollonian. However, as a vision of the true *telos* of human existence, the fountains that Maderna set before St. Peter's are even more mystical than they are Apollonian. The water's trajectory is an allegory for the ascent of a human soul—struggling perhaps through spiritual discipline, until it is "at rest" in a pattern of rising toward God. "The very wish of the water," that is, the natural (gravitational) "desire" to be earthly, is overcome, and the head is "clear, high" and "cavorting" in heavenly play, filled with the blaze of God's glory. As in some mystical experiences, the self is transformed into "a fine / Illumined version of itself."

This description, like that of the baroque fountain, contains within itself seeds of doubt that it is entirely satisfactory as a vision of human nature. For example, in contrast to "Teresa," where sexual imagery communicated the involvement of Teresa's whole self (including the erotic) in dedication to

God,[18] in this section of "A Baroque Wall Fountain" the phallic imagery seems to suggest that in an orgasmic blaze the body disappears. To what end? The genuine mystic would answer, "to participate in God's glory." But, here, it is possible that the body's disappearance finally may be self-indulgent. The "fine / Illumined version of itself" will "patter on the stones its own applause." Furthermore, also in contrast to Teresa whose spirituality led her to run "God's barefoot errands in the rocks of Spain," here there is no suggestion that mystical rapture leads to engagement with the world. The vision of human nature expressed in the fountains in front of St. Peter's does not add spirituality to the secular scene or lead unambiguously to purification. It removes the secular and physical, replacing them with a vision of what is truly human that is entirely spiritualized, and possibly self-indulgent.

The final stanzas of this poem reveal that Wilbur is indeed uncomfortable in seeking a mystical escape into pure spirituality. He remains haunted by the baroque fountain:

> If that is what men are
> Or should be, if those water saints display
>   The pattern of our areté,
> What of these showered fauns in their bizarre,
>
>   Spangled, and plunging house?
> They are at rest in fulness of desire
>   For what is given, they do not tire
> Of the smart of the sun, the pleasant water-douse
>
>   And riddled pool below,
> Reproving our disgust and our ennui
>   With humble insatiety.
> Francis, perhaps, who lay in sister snow
>
>   Before the wealthy gate
> Freezing and praising, might have seen in this

---

[18]See Chapter One, 19-23.

No trifle, but a shade of bliss–
That land of tolerable flowers, that state

As near and far as grass
Where eyes become the sunlight, and the hand
Is worthy of water: the dreamt land
Towards which all hungers leap, all pleasures pass.

If mystical ecstasy, if losing the self in a blaze of God's glory, is what humanity should be committed to, the poet asks, what shall we make of the attractive characteristics present in the baroque fountain? What of accepting one's creatureliness? What of accepting God's gifts without "disgust" or "ennui"? What of being "at rest–in fulness of desire / For what is given" rather than at rest in striving for what is beyond?

The meditative voice in this poem finally seeks to resolve the dramatic conflict. With some tentativeness, Wilbur puts forward yet another view of humanity. His model is St. Francis–both spiritual and committed to creation, living fully in this fallen world and yet focused on the next. St. Francis does not deny pain but accepts this world as a "shade of bliss." Not paradise, this world yet enables him to know the world to come. Snow, flowers, grass, sunlight, and water: truly one with these, he is at heaven's gate. His experience of paradise is imaginative and proleptic.

It turns out, then, that the choice which the poem leaves with us is not so much between accepting the things of this world and trying to escape as between relating to the things of this world in the manner of St. Francis or settling for something less: spiritless sensuality or disembodied mysticism. The dramatic tension is resolved as the Franciscan vision emerges. As Martz's description of interior dramatization would have it, the poet has recorded the creation of "a self that is . . . one with itself, . . . with created nature, and with the supernatural." Partial visions of the self have been projected onto a stage and brought into dialogue with the whole self. A new self or at least a greater self-understanding has emerged from the process.

Wit is another characteristic of Wilbur's work which marks him as a meditative poet. In fact, the definitions of wit in standard reference works could almost stand as descriptions of one element of Wilbur's style. For example, there is M.H. Abrams' definition of wit that is rooted in metaphysical poetry: "ingenuity in literary invention, . . . especially . . . the ability to discover brilliant, surprising, and paradoxical figures."[19] C. Hugh Holman suggests that "It is for the most part agreed that *wit* is primarily intellectual, the perception of similarities in seemingly dissimilar things-the 'swift play and flash of mind,'-and is expressed in skillful phraseology, plays upon words, surprising contrasts, paradoxes, epigrams, comparison, etc."[20]

Wilbur's playfulness with language prompts some critics to respond to his work captiously. There is, however, nothing in the nature of wit that prevents its being employed for serious purposes, as the English metaphysical tradition (Donne, Herbert, Vaughn) amply indicates. In this connection, Bruce Michelson calls Wilbur's work "festivity for the sake of seriousness," invoking Huizinga's authority to define play as-"in its highest state . . . the exuberant celebration of mystery." Michelson looks back over Wilbur's career and concludes that "Wilbur has spent thirty years . . . showing us that wit and passionate intensity can have everything to do with one another."[21]

Wit is used by Wilbur to surprise his readers, to jostle their preconceptions, and open their minds to more than their eyes can see. That is, he uses wit as a strategy by which transcendence is revealed. On a few occasions, Wilbur's wit assumes the form of an extended conceit, as in the poem "Complaint" from *Walking to Sleep* (*WS:NCP* 123-4).[22] The speaker is a "bumbling servant" who confesses, "After twenty years of struggling to be

---

[19]M.H. Abrams, *A Glossary of Literary Terms*, 3rd ed. (New York: Holt, Rinehart and Winston, Inc., 1971), 179.

[20]C. Hugh Holman, *A Handbook to Literature: Based on the Original by William Flint Thrall and Addison Hibbard*, 3rd ed. (Indianapolis: The Bobbs-Merrill Company, Inc., 1972), 558.

[21]Bruce Michelson, "Wilbur's Words," in Salinger, 175. Michelson, "Richard Wilbur's *The Mind-Reader*," in Salinger, 132. See also Johan Huizinga, *Homo Ludens: A Study of the Play Element in Culture* (Boston: Beacon Press, 1955), 4-11, 46, and Jürgen Moltmann, "Three Lectures on the Theology of Hope," *Kalamazoo College Review* 32, no. 3 (1970): 18-24.

[22]Another is "The Beacon" (*TTW:NCP* 249-50).

a courtier / I remain incapable of the least politeness, / Wit, song, or learning." His fantasies bring him to the duchess he adores as three very distinct and fascinating personalities: a sea captain, a court jester, and a priest. In each he wins her love and attention. And each is an indictment of the servant's real self. The servant's complaint ends where it began, in wistful longing and resigned devotion:

> Why is it that whenever I talk with the duchess
> My belly growls and my nose waters? Why must it
> Be my hand that tumbles her wine-glass over
> Into the Cellini salt-dish?
>
> Stiff as a gaffer, fidgety as a child,
> After twenty years of struggling to be a courtier
> I remain incapable of the least politeness,
> Wit, song, or learning,
>
> And I wonder sometimes, what is it in me that hates me?
> Is it that rolling captain who should burst
> Like surf into her presence, dumping down
> His pillage of the seas,
>
> And in a wink dissolve her castled pride?
> She scorns no common magic, and could be pleased
> To be manhandled like a kitchen-girl,
> So it were sweet and reckless.
>
> Or is it that idolatrous fool that's in me,
> Who, lest she alter, should enchant the hour
> With gentled sparrows and an aimless lute,
> Enthralling her with tales
>
> Of a king's daughter bound in mountain sleep,
> Whose prince and wakener, detained by trials

In deserts, deeps, and grottoes of the world,
Approaches her forever?

Or am I spited by the priest I might be
There in the stone grove of her oratory?
No ship sails out so free as she at prayer,
With head bowed and shrouded.

Confessing her, and my delight in her,
To the great ways and haven of her beauty,
Would I not serve her better? Would not my hand
Be steady with the wine?

Jackass, again you turn and turn this prism,
Whose every light is of the purest water.
How should I fathom her whose white hands fold
The rainbow like a fan?

O maiden, muse, and maiden, O my love
Whose every moment is the quick of time,
I am your bumbling servant now and ever,
In this and the other kingdom.

The servant's ascription of the title "muse" to his duchess in the final stanza suggests that he is a frustrated poet who feels mocked by his lack of success and daydreams about three kinds of relationships to his muse. In other words, he sees the possibility of being a poet whose imagination dominates the world. He could act like a sea captain who pillages the world for material to manipulate into acceptable forms. Or, he could write poetry like a court jester, a poet whose fancy entertains others but seeks no deep meaning from life, a teller of tales to "enchant the hour." Or, finally, he could be reverentially attentive to his muse, waiting as a patient priest to hear her disclosures when she freely offers them. Yet he remains a bumbling writer. Unlike "A Baroque Wall Fountain" this poem refuses to suggest a resolution to the speaker's dilemma. Hence, the epigraph from Ficino: *"In reality, each love is that of the divine image, and each is pure."* Each love is pure, including the "unsuccessful" love of the would-be courtier/poet.

If this reading of "Complaint" is cogent, then the poem is quite fine on two separate levels and brilliant in the witty construction of the conceit which unites them. As the complaint of a would-be courtier, the poem invites readers to a bemused consideration of unfulfilled desire. The tone is that of self-deprecating humor, with potential bitterness mellowed by long years of practiced resignation. The poem takes on a greater degree of sharpness as the complaint of a poet struggling with a perfectionist conscience and the necessary choices in poetics. Readers who are not poets may even see this poem as an allegory of themselves. They too may be frustrated by imperfection in their professional performance and tempted to ride roughshod over people and things, to skate on the surface of issues, or resignedly to elect a kind of "celibate" distance and passivity. Contrary to the assumption made by some of Wilbur's critics (that his intellect gets in the way of the reader's emotional engagement with his poems), the conceit at work here does not make the poem less personal for introspective readers, but more so.

A key constituent of Wilbur's wit is his extensive vocabulary, a common characteristic of meditative poets:

> The self of meditative poetry speaks a language based on that of common men, but including whatever in its own experience is unique and individual. If the self is learned and theological in its bent, then common speech will be infused with learned, theological terms and ways of thought.[23]

Wilbur's word choice relies heavily on etymological and allusive considerations. This practice has come under fire from hostile critics who find his vocabulary too cerebral to be vital. In a symposium at the College of Wooster in 1966, Wilbur seems to be defending himself:

> It must be admitted that the poet's fascination with words can degenerate into fetishism and the pursuit of the exotic. More often, however, such researches are the necessary, playful groundwork for that serious business of naming which I have been discussing. . . . Every poet is impelled to utter the whole of that world which is real to him. . . . The job is an

---

[23]Martz, *The Poetry of Meditation*, 323.

endless one, because there are some aspects of life that we acknowledge to
be real, but have not yet truly accepted. (R 97-98)

However, instead of bargaining for the right to be esoteric, Wilbur
went on to advocate including all aspects of the *common* in poetry. He
concluded:

> One perpetual task of the poet is to produce models of inclusive reaction
> and to let no word or thing be blackballed by sensibility. That is why I
> took a large pleasure, some years ago, in bringing off a line that
> convincingly employed the words, "reinforced concrete." . . . For poetry
> there is no such thing as no man's land. (R 98-99)

In two of his essays, "The Genie in the Bottle"[24] and "Round About a
Poem of Housman's" (R 16-38), Wilbur takes positions more in keeping with
his reputation. In these essays, he defends a poet's right to be allusive as well
as inclusive. In the Housman article an argument by Karl Shapiro from
Poetry magazine is used as a foil: "Mr. Shapiro talks as if a poem could be
either referential or humanly vital but not both. Surely you will agree that
Housman's poem ("Epitaph on an Army of Mercenaries") is both . . . . What
he does is confront the present with a mind and heart that contain the past"
(R 30). The argument comes down to Wilbur's affirmation of a poet's
freedom: "It would not be worth it to make poetry more generally usable at
the cost of abridging the poet's consciousness" (R 29).

Wilbur believes, however, that poets will not want to exercise their
freedom to choose a vocabulary that makes their poems inaccessible.
Obscurantism is an impediment to effective poetry:

> A poem should not be a Double-Crostic; it should not be the sort of puzzle
> in which you get nothing until you get it all. Art does not or should not
> work that way; we are not cheated of a symphony if we fail to react to
> some passage on the flute, and a good poem should yield itself more than
> once, offering the reader an early and sure passage, and deepening
> repeatedly as he comes to know it better. (R 31-32)

And, Wilbur follows his own advice: his poetry is rarely esoteric and
never needlessly opaque. True, his work is addressed to the cultivated

---

[24]Richard Wilbur, "The Genie in the Bottle," 1-7 (see chap. 1, n. 8).

reader, and it may at times be taxing; but at no point does it exhibit any sort of willful obscurity.

It is not surprising that Wilbur became a "meditative poet." The English poets in whose work Martz first discerned the genre were precisely those poets whom Wilbur came to respect in his formative years:

> Most American poets of my generation were taught to admire the English metaphysical poets of the seventeenth century and such contemporary masters of irony as John Crowe Ransom. We were led by our teachers and by the critics whom we read to feel that the most adequate and convincing poetry is that which accommodates mixed feelings, clashing ideas, and incongruous images. Poetry could not be honest, we thought, unless it began by acknowledging the full discordancy of modern life and consciousness. (*R* 118-119)

Even though, as Wilbur puts it, his own work has partially shifted "from the ironic meditative lyric toward the dramatic poem" (*R* 118), he still believes that his early opinion is "a true view of poetry" (*R* 119). Indeed, the influence of formal religious meditation is as apparent in his later work as it was in his first volumes of verse. In formal structure and by using interior dramatization and wit, and by using other strategies consistent with meditative poetry (to be described in Chapter Four), Wilbur has consistently written "as one who feels the hand of the supernatural upon himself and upon all created things."[25]

---

[25]Martz, *The Poetry of Meditation*, 324.

Chapter Four

KINETIC STRATEGIES:
POETRY MOVING TOWARD ECSTASY

His is the most kinetic poetry I know.

Anthony Hecht

Wilbur expresses G.M. Hopkins' belief that "the world is charged with the grandeur of God." And because it is so charged, Wilbur's attitude toward life is that of a man humbled by the mystery and magnificence of all he observes. His responsiveness to beauty is not just a sense of aesthetic delight, though this is usually present. It is also inspired by the constant awareness of the Divine at work in the mundane.

Paul F. Cummins

The preceding chapters have maintained that Richard Wilbur may rightly be referred to as a "meditative poet" because of his interests, temperament, and repeated use of formulae associated with the genre of meditative poetry. However, the definition of meditative poetry offered by Louis Martz does not fully encompass the ways in which Wilbur's poetry evokes and expresses ecstatic experience. This chapter describes and illustrates Wilbur's frequent use of three kinetic strategies: close attention, dialectics, and liminality (none of which is treated extensively or systematically by Martz). Habitually, Wilbur gives objects close and then closer attention. And he follows the progress of a "thesis" through its encounters with its "antithesis" to its development into a new "synthesis." Also, he often moves the reader outside of normal patterns of thought and the established structures of society by using liminal characters and settings for his poems. These are three of the ways Wilbur's poems trace paths toward ecstasy, paths which end in wonder at mystery or transcendence.

When Wilbur attends poetically to an object or to an event, his observation is keen. Details are vividly described, and, through close attention, he often perceives the presence of "something more." What we discern in Wilbur's approach is a kind of discipline not unlike that which Nathan Scott (using terminology drawn from Heidegger) descries in the poetry of Theodore Roethke:

> . . . when the world begins no longer to be approached merely as something to be "attacked" in the manner of a technological project, . . .when we consent to approach it in the spirit of what Heidegger calls *Gelassenheit* (that is, surrender, abandonment, acquiescence)—it is only then that the "voice" of Being begins to be heard. . . . Until we have learned again the discipline of "letting-be," we shall not achieve the condition of what Heidegger calls "releasement toward things" which is nothing other than an attitude of simple enthrallment before the sheer concreteness and specificity of all the various givens of the earth. . . . Heidegger speaks of . . . "meditative thinking," . . . "openness" to radical mystery, to the mystery of there being something rather than nothing. Meditative thinking is a thinking in which the originating force proceeds, as it were, not so much from the mind itself as from that under which it stands, so that we feel a claim being laid upon us. . . . The meditative thinker knows himself to be addressed by something transcendent, . . . the knowledge which is brought to him as a result of his "meditation" is something like a gift.[1]

Approaching the natural world "in the spirit of . . . *Gelassenheit*," Wilbur typically begins poems with detailed descriptions of what the senses perceive and ends them with clear affirmations of mystery.[2]

---

[1] Scott, *The Wild Prayer of Longing: Poetry and the Sacred*, 67-68 (see chap. 1, n. 23). There is a *theological* difference between what Scott describes in Heidegger's work and what I perceive in Wilbur's poems. Scott claims that Heidegger's implicit theological position most closely resembles panentheism. Among various theological options, however, Wilbur's poetry is most compatible with traditional Judeo-Christian theism. See Scott, 49-66.

[2] One such poem already examined is "A Hole in the Floor." See Chapter Three, 59-62.

The poem "Cicadas" (*BC:NCP* 337), from Wilbur's first book, is a good example. It moves from considering a natural scene to a consideration of the transcendence it signals:

> You know those windless summer evenings, swollen to stasis
> by too substantial melodies, rich as a
> running-down record, ground round
> to full quiet. Even the leaves
> have thick tongues.

> And if the first crickets quicken then,
> other inhabitants, at window or door
> or rising from table, feel in the lungs
> a slim false-freshness, by this
> trick of the ear.

> Chanters of miracles took for a simple sign
> The Latin cicada, because of his long waiting
> and sweet change in daylight, and his singing
> all his life, pinched on the ash leaf,
> heedless of ants.

> Others made morals; all were puzzled and joyed
> by this gratuitous song. Such a plain thing
> morals could not surround, nor listening:
> not "chirr" nor "cri-cri." There is no straight
> way of approaching it.

> This thin uncomprehended song it is
> springs healing questions into binding air.
> Fabre, by firing all the municipal cannon
> under a piping tree, found out
> cicadas cannot hear.

The poem begins by evoking our memories of summer nights and the feelings stirred by cries of crickets and cicadas. The poem's reflective mood changes, however, in stanza three, as Wilbur begins to enumerate various "theories" about cicadas: theories which happen to represent the four levels of meaning (literal, allegorical, moral, and anagogical) advanced by medieval hermeneutics.[3] Fabre was a literalist. Allegories were made by "chanters of miracles [who] took for a simple sign / the Latin cicada, because of his long waiting / and sweet change in daylight, and his singing / all his life. . . ." "Others," we are told, "made morals." Of all the possible ways to understand the significance of cicadas, the anagogical is the only one adequate to the experience: "Such a plain thing / morals could not surround, nor listening." Wilbur affirms the mystical and ultimately spiritual meaning of the cicada's song: "There is no straight way of approaching it. / This thin uncomprehended song it is / springs healing questions into binding air." The poem's closing lines summarize   the naturalist Fabre's experiments (concluding "cicada's cannot hear") and reinforce the notion that the natural world is mysterious.   Thus, "Cicadas" follows the pattern of religious meditation: setting the scene, analysis, and encountering mystery. And each step involves giving closer attention to the phenomenon of cicadas than the step before.   The poem moves its readers from casual observation through disciplined analysis to contemplative appreciation of the cicada and its song.

The self that can discern the mysteriously healing questions of the cicada's song is fortunate, and, as Wilbur has remarked elsewhere, increasingly rare:

> Certain ways and means of perceiving nature are fast being lost to us. . . .
> Bryant's homiletic woods, Emerson's or Whitman's symbolic streams or grasses, all latter versions and warpings of the old notion that nature is a book of revelations, have lost much credit in this century; the book has grown difficult to read, and when one hears it read in poem or pulpit, it is commonly done with small fidelity or conviction. This is unfortunate for the imagination, which when in best health neither slights the world of fact nor stops with it, but seeks the invisible through the visible. (*R* 158-159)

---

[3] Dante Alighieri, "From 'Letter to Can Grande Della Scalla'" in *Critical Theory Since Plato*, ed. Hazard Adams (New York: Harcourt Brace Jovanovich, Inc., 1971), 121-123. Hill disagrees. He comments on the arbitrariness of Wilbur's selection of details to include in this poem, Hill. 28 (see chap. 2, n. 6).

Many of Wilbur's poems are indeed hermeneutical, recording his interpretations of nature as a book of revelation. In turn, his poems become literary markers for those who choose to select his guidance as they themselves "seek the invisible through the visible."

In "A Wedding Toast" (*MR:NCP* 61), Wilbur is equally explicit about the surplus of meaning present in the everyday world: "Life hungers to abound / And pour its plenty out for such as you." In "Bell Speech" (*BC:NCP* 380), he writes that "bells beseech / By some excess that's in their stricken speech / Less meanly to be heard." There is mystery, something more, which enables the bell to "dip and draw / Dark speech from the deep and quiet steeple well / . . . [and] gather to a language without flaw / Our loves, and all the hours of our death."

In "Thyme Flowering Among Rocks" (*WS:NCP* 142-3), though Wilbur begins with an allusion to Japanese art (and its assumption that there is a spiritual relationship among nature, art, and self), by the third stanza he has anchored his poem in a reality neither esoteric nor abstract:

> This, if Japanese,
> Would represent grey boulders
> Walloped by rough seas
>
> So that, here or there,
> The balked water tossed its froth
> Straight into the air.
>
> Here, where things are what
> They are, it is thyme blooming,
> Rocks, and nothing but –

In the very next stanza, however, facts once again begin to have implications beyond themselves:

> Having, nonetheless
> Many small leaves implicit,
> A green countlessness.

In stanza five the reader is addressed directly ("you") and literally drawn into the scene to wonder at the intricacies of the thyme plant:

> Crouching down, peering
> Into perplexed recesses,
> You find a clearing
>
> Occupied by sun
> Where, along prone rachitic
> Branches, one by one,
>
> Pale stems arise, squared
> In the manner of *Mentha,*
> The oblong leaves paired.
>
> One branch, in ending,
> Lifts a little and begets
> A straight ascending
>
> Spike, whorled with fine blue
> Or purple trumpets, banked in
> The leaf axils. . . .

Finally "you" are drawn into the sense of mystery and transcendence being experienced by the poet:

> . . . You
>
> Are lost now in dense
> Fact, fact which one might have thought
> Hidden from the sense,
>
> Blinking at detail
> Peppery as this fragrance,
> Lost to proper scale

As, in the motion
Of striped fins, a bathysphere
Forgets the ocean.

It makes the craned head
Spin. Unfathomed thyme! The world's
A dream, Basho said,

Not because the dream's
A falsehood, but because it's
Truer than it seems.

With each stanza following the syllabic pattern of a Japanese haiku (which, however, is normally unrhymed), the movement from the empirical to the transcendent is unmistakable: in stanza three, "things are what / They are . . . . / and nothing but–"; by stanza five, the reader is "crouching down, peering" and giving closer attention than before to the uniqueness of the thyme plant; by the concluding stanzas, the reader is invited to affirm "Unfathomed thyme," and also the conviction that "The world's / A dream . . . / Not because the dream's / A falsehood, but because it's / Truer than it seems." Beginning with hints of surplusages of meaning, Wilbur, as he concentrates on the sensations themselves (here, visual), is gradually drawn toward a reality transcending the visual; and he ends the poem in ecstasy: i.e., "standing outside" one's usual position vis á vis a thyme plant.

Wilbur's poems sometimes trace a path to ecstatic experience by recording movement from ordinary observation to more rapt and contemplative attentiveness. At other times his poems come to similar ends by means of dialectic. Typically, as the dialectical process unfolds in a Wilbur poem, previously hidden transcendent dimensions of the theses and antitheses are revealed and become the bases for new, synthetic relationships. Wilbur's fine short poem, "Two Voices in a Meadow," (*AP:NCP* 181) may serve as an example. It echoes many of the themes of "A Baroque Wall-Fountain in the Villa Sciarra."[4]

---

[4] See Chapter Three, 63-70.

A Milkweed

Anonymous as cherubs
Over the crib of God,
White seeds are floating
Out of my burst pod.
What power had I
Before I learned to yield?
Shatter me, great wind:
I shall possess the field.

A Stone

As casual as cow-dung
Under the crib of God,
I lie where chance would have me,
Up to the ears in sod.
Why should I move? To move
befits a light desire.
The sill of Heaven would founder,
Did such as I aspire.

The crib of God mentioned in each part of this poem refers specifically
to the manger of Luke's infancy narrative. It could also be a metaphorical
reference to other physical objects in which God is incarnate. Whatever
"holds" God could be God's crib.[5] Since Wilbur has pointed to the presence
of transcendence in so many objects and occasions, it is not unfair to suggest
that Wilbur intends for the crib of God to refer to the whole created order.
The crib of God is what the opposites present in the text have in common.
Around it are the opposites of lightness and heaviness, motion and stasis,

---

[5] Such a notion is at the heart of sacramental and incarnational theology. Even
Luther once referred to the Old Testament law and prophets as the "swaddling clothes and
manger in which [Christ] was wrapped and laid." Quoted in Philip S. Watson's *Let God Be
God: An Interpretation of the Theology of Martin Luther* (Philadelphia: Fortress Press,
1947), 149.

freedom and fate, ambition and humility, as well as the two opposing Christian traditions that the cluster of traits in each half of the poem comes to represent. Each tradition is quite different in how it accounts for the relationship of God's creatures to the givens of life.

The attitude expressed by the milkweed exemplifies Jesus' enigmatic saying that whoever loses his life will save it. Here, as in mysticism and in the spirituality of monastic orders in the Roman church, the path to a fulfilling relationship with God is the path of self-denial, even self-negation. The milkweed's prayer is addressed to the "great wind," God's Holy Spirit, and once the self is shattered by the wind there is union with God. Union with God allows the milkweed to "possess the field," that is, to leave creatureliness behind and become part of the Creator to whom all things belong. The stone follows a different path. It obeys the will of God which it understands to be implicit in fact. The stone speaks the attitude of all those who in humility accept their places in life and make no pretension to divinity. The stone is earthly, "Up to the ears in sod," and more akin to "cow-dung" than "cherubs." The stone is more Calvinist than Roman.

The milkweed and the stone are not flawless, however, for each flirts with the very temptation that could poison its most prominent virtue. Donald Hill notices this latter dynamic, but analyzes it in secular terms: "These voices carry the virtues of flexibility and steadfastness to the point where they approach opportunism and obstinacy."[6] The spiritual temptation for the milkweed is in its prayer to "possess the field." Its temptation is to desire self-aggrandizement. It might use self-negation, not for the sake of others or God, but in order to gain the reward God has promised to those who suffer loss. It is possible, however, that the temptation is being resisted, for the milkweed's prayer to possess the field *may be* a restatement of God's promise to those willing to offer themselves to the Spirit. The stone's temptation is fatalism. The stone is so stuck in the way things are, it will not respond or risk. Its humility verges on self-abnegation, which can be a way to give honor to God, though it here appears to be an evasion of God's gifts of freedom and responsibility in the world. This stone is too "humble" to move for the sake of its neighbors or God. I take the last two lines of the poem to be self-

---

[6] Hill, 140.

deprecation rather than a statement about the fragility of the created order:
"The sill of Heaven would founder, / Did such as I aspire."

The "Milkweed" section of this poem recognizes that spiritual
aspiration may be tainted by pride; the "Stone" section recognizes that
humility may be tainted by fatalism. One might conclude that Wilbur
despairs of spiritual growth. I think it is more likely that Wilbur intends both
paths of spirituality to be attractive. The poem is not cynical about surrender
to the power of the spirit or honest acceptance of creatureliness. Rather, God
has been somehow present (incarnate, in the crib over which the milkweed
floats and under which the stone lies), activating virtues and confronting
temptations. The incarnate presence of God overcomes the dualities in this
poem. There is, then, in Wilbur's view, a faith in the incarnate God which
may synthesize and transcend different traditions of spirituality.

"Under Cygnus" (*WS:NCP* 140) wrestles with the same issues in a
different way.[7] The issue underlying all others in this poem is presented
clearly in the first of its two stanzas:

> Who says I shall not straighten till I bend,
> And must be broken if I hope to mend?
> Did Samson gain by being chained and blind?
> Dark heaven hints at something of the kind,
> Seeing that as we beat toward Hercules
> Our flank is compassed by the galaxy's,
> And we drawn off from our intended course
> By a grand reel of stars whose banded force
> Catching us up, makes light of all our loss,
> And dances us into the Northern Cross.

The question of lines one and two (must one lose one's life to gain it?)
is marvelously reinforced by Wilbur's allusion to Samson's story in *Judges*
16. The story ends with Samson's death, but he has gained in wisdom and
faith. "Dark heaven" (line 4) refers to the locus of divine truth whose "hints"
are dimly perceived in the story of Samson. It also refers literally to outer
space, introducing the lines that follow which recount astronomically correct

---

[7] See also, "The Aspen and the Stream" (*AP:NCP* 205-6).

movements of stars and planets. They, like Sampson, are drawn off their "intended" course by a greater power. Moreover, the astronomical movements cited are linked to Greek mythology in a way that repeats the lessons of Scripture. In the constellation Hercules, the hero holds "a bow in his outstretched hand" and has "just launched an arrow, Sagitta, toward the two birds, Cygnus and Aquila. . . ."[8] "As we beat toward Hercules" (line five)–that is, as we aspire to superhuman strength and dominance, like that which Sampson and Hercules possessed–we are drawn by gravity (the "banded force" of the "grand reel of stars") toward Cygnus. We have aspired to be the hunter (dominant, in control), but our will is broken and we tend toward the position of the hunted. The hunted is a swan (Cygnus), often "taken as a type of faultlessness or excellence." Swans also symbolize poets because they are supposed to sing just before they die.[9] Thus the poet whose excellence may stand for the height of human achievement is mortal. Facing death inspires the poet's most beautiful song, and losing his life in the pursuit of beauty is the poet's true path to wholeness or salvation. Scripture, the stars, Greek mythology, and literary allusions to the swan "dance us into the Northern Cross," the cross being for Christ the conjunction of obedience, humiliation, death, and glorification.

Yet the last lines of the second stanza affirm the self's power, even though all the evidence of stanza one and the first half of stanza two is that the self must be broken by the powers of heaven:

> Well, if I must surrender and be gay
> In the wrong pasture of the Milky Way,
> If in the Cross I must resign my Sword,
> To hang among the trophies of the Lord,
> Let my distinction not consist alone
> In having let myself be overthrown.
> It was my loves and labors, carried high,
> Which drove the flight that heaven turns awry,

---

[8] Daniel H. Menzel, *A Field Guide to the Stars and Planets* (Boston: Houghton Mifflin Company, 1964), 105.

[9] *Oxford English Dictionary*, s.v. "swan."

My dreams which told the stars what they should tell.
Let the swan, dying, sing of that as well.

The dialectic drawn in these lines is sharp and has literary as well as
theological and religious significance. The poem asserts in its penultimate
line that it is the poet who has given meaning to the stars. Tracing truth back
to human invention manifestly controverts the notion that the world has a
truth of its own waiting to be discovered. The title "Under Cygnus" and most
of the lines in this poem suggest that humanity is best portrayed as caught in
a reality more powerful than its own will. Human intentions are inevitably
drawn off course. The strength of the penultimate line, however, undermines
that conclusion. If we have imaginatively created the power that controls our
destiny, then we ourselves are ultimately in control. The poem, therefore,
does not clearly opt for one choice or the other. Instead we are left with a
dialectic which affirms both humanity's dominion, responsibility, and freedom
on the one hand, and, on the other, the "Lord's" sovereignty (see stanza two,
line four). As in "Two Voices in a Meadow," I do not think that the
dialectical tension leaves the matter unresolved, but rather places us in the
presence of a mystery in which both contraries seem true. It is the same
mystery found in *Genesis*, where humanity is given dominion over all the
earth yet remains one among God's creatures.

This issue, of course, is not the only one treated dialectically by
Wilbur. Ecstasy and discipline are treated dialectically in "Teresa"
(*MR:NCP* 79). "Ceremony" (*C:NCP* 334) synthesizes formality and chaos,
civilization and wilderness. "A Christmas Hymn" (*AP:NCP* 225-6)
celebrates the reconciliation of heaven and earth in the incarnation. These and
others of Wilbur's poems live in the tension of dialectic, but also imply or
assert that the tension is not ultimate reality. It exists in the context of
mystery, a transcendent context which nearly always is grace-filled and
productive of wonder.

The final strategy by which Wilbur brings his readers into awareness
of transcendence is like his strategies of close attention and dialectic in that it
depends on a perception of divisions in reality. When Wilbur pays such
close attention to the things of this world that his observation becomes
contemplation, transcendence gradually becomes manifest in his awareness.

When he uses dialectic, Wilbur notes a transcendent ground or mode for the relationship of opposites. In this last strategy, however, he focuses the reader's attention less on dualities and more on the territory between. It is a strategy which makes use of mediational figures, borderline situations and liminal states.

"Liminality" is a term used by the late anthropologist, Victor Turner. His definition of liminality is instructive:

> Liminality is a term borrowed from Arnold van Gennep's formulation of *rites de passage*, "transition rites"-which accompany every change of state or social position, or certain points in age. These are marked by three phases: separation, margin (or limen-the Latin for threshold, signifying the great importance of real or symbolic thresholds at this middle period of the rites, though cunicular, "being in a tunnel," would better describe the quality of this phase in many cases, its hidden nature, its sometimes mysterious darkness), and reaggregation.
>
> The first phase, separation, comprises symbolic behavior signifying the detachment of the individual or the group from either an earlier fixed point in the social structure or from an established set of social conditions (a "state"). During the intervening liminal period, the state of the ritual subject (the "passenger," or "liminar,") becomes ambiguous, neither here nor there, betwixt and between all fixed points of classification; he passes through a symbolic domain that has few or none of the attributes of his past or coming state. In the third phase the passage is consummated and the ritual subject, the neophyte or initiand reenters the social structure, often but not always at a higher status level.[10]

In a most helpful and suggestive way, Turner has applied the term "liminality" to other non-ritual occasions. An occasion is liminal if one stands aside from one's normal place, whether it be in relation to a social hierarchy, a culture's worldview, or a religious orthodoxy. For example, Turner points to the arts as "'liminoid' analogues of liminal . . . phenomena in tribal and agrarian societies." The arts are among the "genres of free-time activity" which have great "potential for changing the ways men relate to one another and the content of their relationships."[11] In other words, the arts,

---

[10] Victor Turner, *Dramas, Fields, and Metaphors: Symbolic Action in Human Society* (Ithaca: Cornell University Press, 1974), 231-232.

[11] Turner, 15-16.

including poetry, allow us to stand outside the normal patterns of our culture and creatively formulate a new future.

Several of Richard Wilbur's poems illustrate important characteristics of liminality as it is treated in Turner's essays. First, Wilbur's personages are often those whom Turner speaks of as "outsiders," such figures as "shamans, diviners, mediums, priests, those in monastic seclusion, hippies, hoboes, and gypsies."[12] Second, Wilbur's work often affirms the unity of persons with one another and with nature. Turner states that in liminality the "structural status" separating persons from one another and from nature is broken down. "*Communitas*" is possible among persons and also, the human individual "becomes the . . . fellow of nonhuman beings."[13] Third, Turner writes:

> As is well known, theranthropic figures combining animal with human characteristics abound in liminal situations; similarly human beings imitate the behavior of different species of animals. Even angels . . . may perhaps be regarded this way–as ornithanthropic figures, bird-humans, messengers betwixt and between absolute and relative reality.[14]

"Beasts" (about a werewolf *TTW:NCP* 263-4) and "The Undead" (about vampires *AP:NCP* 196-7) are among Wilbur's theranthropic poems. His poem "Advice to a Prophet" (*AP:NCP* 182-3) might also be considered theranthropic, because it suggests that humanity finds its defining characteristics in nature: "What should we be without / The dolphin's arc, the dove's return, / These things in which we have seen ourselves and spoken?"[15] Angels ("ornithanthropic figures") also appear in Wilbur's work   (for example, in "Love Calls Us to the Things of This World" *TTW:NCP* 233-4) and birds are often notable in his poems as mediators between earth and heaven.   Fourth, in Wilbur's work liminality provides a context which illuminates the relationship between the human and the transcendent.   As

---

[12] Turner, 233.

[13] Turner, 250-253. However, contrary to Turner's suggestion that "enhanced stress on nature [comes] at the expense of culture," Wilbur's work embodies "high culture" at the same time as it attends to the natural world.

[14] Turner, 253.

[15] See Chapter Two, 42-45.

Turner says, "Major liminal situations are occasions on which a society *takes cognizance of itself,* or rather where, in an interval between their incumbency of specific fixed positions, members of that society may obtain an approximation, however limited, to a global view of man's place in the cosmos and his relations with other classes of visible and invisible entities."[16]

"Still, Citizen Sparrow" (*C:NCP* 318) is a fine example of a poem of liminality. It uses bird-human figures. It invites its readers to envision a new future and a new "place in the cosmos," as it also invites them to participate in a liminal event mediated by an "outsider" acting as a guide:

Still, citizen sparrow, this vulture which you call
Unnatural, let him but lumber again to air
Over the rotten office, let him bear
The carrion ballast up, and at the tall

Tip of the sky lie cruising. Then you'll see
That no more beautiful bird is in heaven's height,
No wider more placid wings, no watchfuller flight;
He shoulders nature there, the frightfully free,

The naked-headed one. Pardon him, you
Who dart in the orchard aisles, for it is he
Devours death, mocks mutability,
Has heart to make an end, keeps nature new.

Thinking of Noah, childheart, try to forget
How for so many bedlam hours his saw
Soured the song of birds with its wheezy gnaw,
And the slam of his hammer all the day beset

The people's ears. Forget that he could bear
To see the towns like coral under the keel,

---

[16] Turner, 239-240.

And the fields so dismal deep. Try rather to feel
How high and weary it was, on the waters where

He rocked his only world, and everyone's.
Forgive the hero, you who would have died
Gladly with all you knew; he rode that tide
To Ararat; all men are Noah's sons.

This poem is open to several interpretations. Donald Hill claims it has a political context and is meant to honor the isolated figure who heroically takes on society's responsibilities.[17] Paul F. Cummins suggests that the poem celebrates the moral virtue of those who do good while being misunderstood by society.[18] To me, this poem appears to be the presentation of a new perspective on the world and its events to be gained by entering the liminal state.

Citizen sparrow is the one to be instructed by the poem. As citizen, the sparrow is concerned with the ordering of earthly affairs. His characteristic activity is to "dart in the orchard aisles." That is, he spends his time busily absorbed in the cultivated, civilized realm intent on everyday tasks (not in the wildness of a forest or above it all where the vulture cruises). "Childheart" in line one of stanza four may be the sparrow or the reader (who is now addressed directly rather than metaphorically as citizen sparrow). In either case, the addressee is still the one with limited vision. "Childheart" would be obsessed, the poem says, with the trivial annoyance of Noah's noisy building project, oblivious to its significance for the future or its spiritual import. As the first three stanzas invite the sparrow to step outside his normal way of looking at the world to see what the vulture sees, the last three stanzas invite the childheart to assume the perspective of Noah. Both the vulture and Noah are liminal figures who leave behind the structures and assumptions of day-to-day life. They rise above this world and see it in a new way from "heaven's height" or "high and weary . . . on the water." The cost of this new vision is alienation from the likes of citizen sparrow and

---

[17] Hill, 71-72.

[18] Cummins, 31. (See chap. 2, n. 1)

childheart. The vulture is called "unnatural" and Noah, too, is alienated–
"The slam of his hammer all the day beset / The people's ears" before, of
course, he left his neighbors behind to drown.

The perspective of the vulture and of Noah is that of the liminar who
occupies a position between earth and heaven, death and life. Like a priest,
the vulture's "office" involves funereal duties: with a peace that passes
understanding the vulture escorts the dead to heaven, bearing "the carrion
ballast up." Like a priest, the vulture is "frightfully free," sharing in the
frightening freedom of holiness, beyond morality. The vulture eucharistically
"devours death," "mocks mutability," and mediates nature's renewal. Like a
priest, Noah's first responsibility is obedience to God, even if it means being
misunderstood by his neighbors. Like a priest, Noah takes on God's
perspective, gazing with God at the lost world–"he could bear / To see the
towns like coral under the keel, / And the fields so dismal deep." Finally,
Noah mediates the possibility of becoming "Noah's sons," of hearing God's
commands and, at great cost, receiving the gift of life to pass on to the next
generation. The poet asks the sparrow, the childheart, and his readers to
"forgive the hero," to appreciate the liminal perspective, the frightful freedom
it brings, and the benefits these priestly figures mediate for the world. Donald
Hill calls this poem "modern, urbane, casual, reasonable in argument."[19] I
find it just the opposite–a powerful articulation of a point of view alien to
modern consciousness, infused with religious passion, urgently calling its
readers out of "reason" and into liminality, where earth and heaven, death and
life, are mysteriously unified.

Sometimes the liminal in Wilbur's work is located on the border
between night and day, as in"Love Calls Us to The Things of This World"
(*TTW:NCP* 233-4) and "For Ellen" (*BC:NCP* 388). "Walking to Sleep"
(*WS:NCP* 158-61) takes place, in part, in the semi-consciousness of the
transition between wakefulness and sleep. "The Death of a Toad" (*C:NCP*
320) happens on the border of the garden and lawn, where animate and
inanimate objects resemble one another, life flows into death, and this world
shades into another kingdom. "Water-Walker" (*BC:NCP* 338-41) refers to
caddis flies "who breathe / Air and know water" and they define the kind of

---

[19] Hill, 71.

liminality experienced by others in the poem: "Paulsaul the Jew born in Tarshish," who "carried Jew visions to Greeks," and the persona who "cannot go home, nor can leave," who sits on porches (neither in nor out). Finally, nearly two dozen of Wilbur's poems take place, at least in part, on a shoreline or river's bank, where earth and water meet.

Paul F. Cummins is surely right when he states: "Wilbur expresses G.M. Hopkins' belief that 'the world is charged with the grandeur of God.'"[20] However, in Wilbur's view, God's grandeur is not so obvious that the casual observer of nature or the human scene will take note. Even though spiritual insights are most often experienced as gifts of grace, coming at surprising moments and in wondrous ways, Wilbur's poetry is written from a point of view that assumes some kind of preparatory activity to be necessary before insight comes. Many of Wilbur's poems are structured so as to reveal the strategy by which he came to receive the insights he is reporting. Sometimes he follows the steps of traditional religious meditation, writing in the genre of meditative poetry. At other times he expands that tradition by adopting the strategies I have described in this chapter—recording in his poems the movement from casual to intense attentiveness, recording the movement of the dialectical process, and taking on perspectives associated with liminality. All these strategies have been used by Wilbur throughout his career, and all are dynamic. Movement is indeed a hallmark of Wilbur's poems, particularly those which are "inspired by . . . awareness of the Divine at work in the mundane."[21]

It is

> As if we were perceived
> From a black ship
> A small knot of island folk,
> The Light-Dwellers, pouring

---

[20] Cummins, 26.

[21] Cummins, 26.

A life to the dark sea—
All that we do
Is touched with ocean, yet we remain
On the shore of what we know.
"For Dudley" *WS:NCP* 135)

Chapter Five

SEEKING THE INVISIBLE THROUGH THE VISIBLE: CELEBRATIVE, METAPHYSICAL POETRY

Now there is, I conceive, one duality that underlies a great deal of poetry, especially the kind of poetry that is called (aptly, I think) 'metaphysical': it is, in largest terms, the duality of the One and the Many. Metaphysical poetry is a poetry of the dilemma, and the dilemma which paradoxes and antitheses continually seek to display is the famous one at which all philosophies falter, the relation of the One with the Many, the leap by which infinity becomes finite, essence becomes existence; the commingling of the spirit with matter, the working of God in the world.

Howard Nemerov

The opposites which need to come together for a celebration are of many kinds; heart and head, feeling and thinking; conscious and unconscious, critical intellect and intuitive intellect; experience of time, experience of eternity; individual and group, personal and social; myself and the world. For celebration the gulf between objective and subjective needs to be bridged. We have to go beyond this cramping distinction, which is so obstructive to our understanding of persons, and find ourselves in a more intimate, coinherent relationship with others and the world around us. . . . There is a reciprocity, an interaction, a co-inherence, between man and man, between man and nature, between man and God, in which distinction is not destroyed, but separateness is overcome, in which the opposites come together into one, and celebrate. . . . There indeed we may find that we may be liberated in our perceptions so that we may see this world not only insofar as it suits our purposes, but as it is in itself, when it is known as the work of a merciful creator, "more alive, more personal, more resonant with unity, more terrifying, full of variety, of complexity and of astonishing surprise."

A.M. Allchin

The preceding chapters focus on *how* Wilbur's poems utilize the formal resources of poetry to describe, evoke, and express mystery and transcendence as they are resident in the material world. Chapter One points out that Wilbur is linked more closely than many critics have noticed to the "Wordsworthian" Romantic tradition and to the innovations of American poetics at mid-century. Chapter Two summarizes important epistemological assumptions which give shape to Wilbur's poetry. The formal options he chooses are those that are consonant with his notions about the world's character, the capabilities of perceiving minds, and the nature of human community. Chapters Three and Four describe several strategies by which Wilbur effectively carries his readers along, "seeking the invisible through the visible" (*R* 159). Finally, in this chapter, the focus shifts to Wilbur's vision itself: specifically, to the relationship of transcendence and materiality. The epigraphs from Howard Nemerov and A.M. Allchin were chosen to suggest that Wilbur's vision is metaphysical and celebrative. His work is, indeed, about the "duality of the One and the Many."[1] His poems bring together "the opposites which need to come together for a celebration."[2]

Wilbur has not responded to this world's dualities, however, by devising any sort of philosophical or theological system. He remains an exploratory poet moving among the things of this world with a tentativeness born of reverence, keenly observant and deeply thoughtful. Nevertheless, even though on fine points and specific issues Wilbur's work does not display the precision or consistency necessary for him to be associated with any one mentor, philosophical school, or theological movement, he is *oriented* philosophically and theologically. Other critics have attempted to describe his orientation in relation to Hopkins, Eliot, Stevens, and Teilard de Chardin.

---

[1] Howard Nemerov, quoted by Reed Whittemore, "Verse," in Salinger, 43.

[2] A..M. Allchin, *The World Is A Wedding: Explorations in Christian Spirituality* (New York: The Crossroad Publishing Company, 1982), 56.

I turn for comparison and contrast to Emerson, Frost, Christian Scripture, Thomas Merton, and Emily Dickinson.

It is tempting, though finally misleading, to think of Wilbur's poems as examples of an Emersonian solution to the problem of the One and the Many. To be sure, there is a rough resemblance in Wilbur's work to Emerson's combination of delight in the particular and affirmation of a unifying transcendental spirit. In "Hamatreya," for example, Emerson's transcendentalism is expressed by the image of the earth swallowing up the individuality of his neighbors when they die. But, in the same poem, Emerson cannot help reveling in the vitality of his neighbors' names and crops. The poem begins:

> Bulkely, Hunt, Willard, Hosmer, Meriam, Flint
> Possessed the land which rendered to their toil
> Hay, corn, roots, hemp, flax, apples, wool and wood.[3]

By the end of "Hamatreya," Emerson's role as pedagogue overshadows his role as celebrant, and the lesson is clear: one ought not to love the things of this world too much, for death will put an end to all possessing. One's proper relationship to land and trees and corn and apples is achieved by one's keeping at a certain distance from them.

Emerson's prescription for distance between persons and things stems from his idealism. He creates a hierarchy of that which he values: material objects and the whole natural world are subordinate to mind and spirit.[4] Consequently, the activity Emerson values most is the intercourse of an individual's mind with the universal spirit unencumbered by substantiality: "The best moments of life are these delicious awakenings of the higher powers and the reverential withdrawing of nature before God."[5] Nature

---

[3] "Hamatreya," in *Selections from Ralph Waldo Emerson*, ed. Stephen E. Whicher (Boston: Houghton Mifflin Company, 1957), 437.

[4] Within the mind, Emerson particularly values "Reason." The spirit he writes of is "universal" and "within or behind . . . individual life." "Nature" in Whicher, 32.

[5] Emerson, 43.

ranks third in Emerson's value system, below spirit and reason, and its role is
to serve them. "It receives the dominion of man as meekly as the ass on
which the savior rode."[6] Nature serves, first, by providing humanity with the
means for commercial and creative productivity, and, second, by providing
occasions of beauty.[7] Third, nature is a vehicle for the development of
human language: "Every word which is used to express a moral or
intellectual fact, if traced to its root, is found to be borrowed from some
material appearance."[8] And fourth, nature's "public and universal function"
is to teach ethics.[9] Referring to these four functions, Emerson concludes:
"All the uses of nature admit of being summed in one. . . . It always speaks
of Spirit. It suggests the absolute. . . . It is the organ through which the
universal spirit speaks to the individual, and strives to lead back the
individual to it."[10] This is a noble function for nature, and though it is
subordinate to spirit and reason in Emerson's system, nature is not despised:
"I have no hostility to nature," he exclaims, "but a child's love to it."[11] The
child's relationship to nature is idealized by Emerson[12] because children are
so intuitive. Adults should strive to recapture the capabilities they left behind
in childhood.[13] Most often, however, adults fall prey to the temptation to use
what Wordsworth termed the "meddling intellect."[14] They dissect and

---

[6] Emerson, 38.

[7] Emerson, 25-31.

[8] Emerson, 31.

[9] Emerson, 39.

[10] Emerson, 49.

[11] Emerson, 48.

[12] Emerson, 53. See also Tony Tanner, *The Reign of Wonder: Naivety and
Reality in American Literature* (New York: Harper and Row, 1967), 5-8, 21, 32-33,
44.

[13] See Emerson, "Mottoes: Nature," 459.

classify while forgetting nature's true purposes. Or they get so caught up in the functions of nature (to mediate commercial productivity, beauty, language, and ethics), they lose track of their final and spiritual *telos.* Emerson tells his readers how to avoid these temptations: "The soul holds itself off from a too trivial and microscopic study of the universal tablet. It respects the [spiritual] end too much to immerse itself in the [material] means."[15]

Wilbur's poetry departs from Emersonian thought at several points. First, Wilbur's view of nature is less oriented to utility and function than Emerson's. For Wilbur, nature is good because of what it is, not because of what it does. I must admit that the personae of Wilbur's poems derive benefits from attention to nature that are related to Emerson's conceptions: "Advice to a Prophet" (*AP:NCP* 182-3), for example, sounds Emersonian as it counsels renewing one's sense of the correspondence between words and natural phenomena in order to revivify language. And, in "The Eye" (*MR:NCP* 56-7), cleansed vision yields spiritual wholeness in a way that echoes Emerson's famous passage about becoming "a transparent eyeball."[16] But in Wilbur's poems such benefits are side effects: one's relationship to nature is intrinsically valuable. Emerson's vision is utilitarian. That is, for Emerson, the value of one's relationship to nature *depends* on its usefulness.

Moreover, Wilbur has a democratic rather than a hierarchical view of his own faculties. Which is to say that, though he relies most often on his sight, he also values whatever evidence comes through his other senses, as well as through memory, intuition, and intellect. Emerson made it a principle to subordinate sensuality to reason, whereas Wilbur's intention is to be holistic and balanced. And the most important distinction to be drawn between the perspectives of Wilbur and Emerson is that Wilbur does not share Emerson's idealism. In Wilbur's vision the spiritual is incarnate in the

---

[14] "The Tables Turned" in *Selected Poems and Prefaces by William Wordsworth*, ed., Jack Stillinger (Boston: Houghton Mifflin Company, 1965), 107.

[15] Emerson, 48.

[16] Emerson, 24.

physical and cannot be abstracted from it. The spiritual and the material are so intimately related that each could not be what it is without the other as a dimension of itself. Whereas Emerson pursued a spirituality that eventually leaves the physical world behind, Wilbur "favors a spirituality that is not abstracted, not dissociated and world-renouncing" (*R* 125). Finally, when Emerson and Wilbur discern the same spiritual peril (losing one's sense of the spiritual by becoming too restrictive in one's approach to nature), they suggest nearly opposite remedies. Emerson directs the soul to "hold itself off from a too timid and microscopic study of the universal tablet," taking care *not* to "immerse" itself in nature and thereby lose sight of its spiritual goal.[17] Wilbur, on the other hand, suggests (in "Advice to a Prophet") that the antidote to trivializing nature by merely quantifying it is to immerse oneself even more deeply in the natural world. In Wilbur's view, transcendence is evident to the eye which gradually becomes more keen and the heart which grows in sympathy for nature. By sensing that there is more peril to one's soul in abstraction than in involvement with the physical world, Wilbur reveals himself to be at odds with a key precept in Emerson's philosophy and allied with the intuitions of the most creative minds of his own generation.

Wilbur's poetry is more like Robert Frost's than Emerson's when the comparison centers on how they approach the duality of the One and the Many or the relationship of spirit and fact. Frost was an influential figure at Amherst College when Wilbur was a student there, and they remained friends for the rest of Frost's life. His influence on Wilbur is especially evident when Frost's poem "Putting in the Seed" is considered in relation to Wilbur's companion piece, "Seed Leaves."[18] Frost's poem places within one of his rustic characters the very conflict which most patently divides the perspectives of Wilbur and Emerson, for he presents the conflict between a seductive call to lose oneself in the abstraction of "a springtime passion for

---

[17] Emerson, 48.

[18] "Putting in the Seed" in *The Poetry of Robert Frost*, ed. Edward Connery Lathem (New York: Holt, Rinehart and Winston, 1969), 123-124. I am indebted to Professor J.C. Levenson who first brought to my attention the relationship of this poem and "Seed Leaves."

the earth" and a call to supper, food for the planter's very particular and substantial body:

> You come to fetch me from my work tonight
> When supper's on the table, and we'll see
> If I can leave off burying the white
> Soft petals fallen from the apple tree
> (Soft petals, yes, but not so barren quite,
> Mingled with these, smooth bean and wrinkled pea),
> And go along with you ere you lose sight
> Of what you came for and become like me,
> Slave to a springtime passion for the earth.
> How Love burns through the Putting in the Seed
> On through the watching for that early birth
> When, just as the soil tarnishes with weed,
> The sturdy seedling with arched body comes
> Shouldering its way and shedding the earth crumbs.

It is not readily apparent which course the speaker will choose, for in this poem the dilemma is displayed rather than resolved. Generally, however, Frost's preference is for the particular and substantial over the abstract. His preference is clearly stated in other poems which appear alongside "Putting in the Seed" in his 1916 volume, *Mountain Interval*—such poems as "Bond and Free" and "Birches." In "Birches," the speaker says:

> I'd like to get away from earth awhile
> And then come back to it and begin over.
> May no fate willfully misunderstand me
> And half grant what I wish and snatch me away
> Not to return. Earth's the right place for love:
> I don't know where it's likely to go better.[19]

---

[19] Frost, 122.

"Birches," Wilbur has pointed out, alludes to Percy Shelley's *Adonais* and "is in fact an answer to Shelley's kind of boundless neo-Platonic aspiration. . . . In *Adonais*, Shelley, spurning the Earth, is embarking on a one-way upward voyage to the Absolute. 'Birches' is contending . . . in favor of another version of spirituality." Wilbur describes the spirituality in "Birches" as "high-minded earthliness" (*R* 112-114). "Putting in the Seed," however, suggests that the choice is not as simple as deciding whether one's quest is upward or downward, for, even while attending to the earth, one may lose touch with it. In the manner of Emerson and other idealists, in line ten Frost uses capitals to emphasize "How *Love* burns through the *Putting* in the *Seed*." He indicates thereby that it is no longer the physical act of burying white petals with beans and peas that would make the speaker skip supper, but passionate involvement with the ideal. This is an ideal born of the physical act of planting, but, as in Emersonianism, the physical has become secondary. When all is said and done, "Putting in the Seed" is the depiction of a temptation which would wrest one from the earth. It does not tell how one might celebrate a right relationship with it.

This is the implication of Wilbur's poem "Seed Leaves" (*WS:NCP* 129-30), which takes up where Frost's poem leaves off, and is a commentary on it. The last two lines of Frost's "Putting in the Seed" are:

> The sturdy seedling with arched body comes
> Shouldering its way and shedding the earth crumbs.

Wilbur's poem has a dedicatory epigraph, "Homage to R.F.," and then begins,

> Here something stubborn comes,
> Dislodging the earth crumbs
> And making crusty rubble.

In Wilbur's poem, the emerging plant has been invested with the spiritual dilemma that faced the planter in "Putting in the Seed." Now the plant is the one tempted to eschew earth-bound particularity and become one with an abstraction. Of course, a plant can make no such choice. It is its

particular self by dint of the nature it was given when its seed was planted.
Wilbur seems to be making the point that the same is true for the planter: he
is who he is by dint of his origins. As a physical being, he is limited to
certain kinds of relationships. He cannot merge with ideal forms, but he can
"commerce" with other particular beings. Before the plant comes to this
conclusion in "Seed Leaves," it suffers through a stage of infantile longing for
oneness with its whole environment. As it matures, the plant learns that it
must relate to the outside world through its own particularity rather than
without it. The plant,

> . . . comes up bending double,
> And looks like a green staple.
> It could be seedling maple
> Or artichoke, or bean.
> That remains to be seen.
>
> Forced to make choice of ends,
> The stalk in time unbends,
> Shakes off the seed-case, heaves
> Aloft, and spreads two leaves
> Which still display no sure
> And special signature.
> Toothless and fat, they keep
> The oval form of sleep.
>
> This plant would like to grow
> And yet be embryo;
> Increase, and yet escape
> The doom of taking shape;
> Be vaguely vast, and climb
> To the tip end of time
> With all of space to fill,
> Like boundless Igdrasil
> That has the stars for fruit.

> But something at the root
> More urgent than that urge
> Bids two true leaves emerge,
> And now the plant, resigned
> To being self-defined
> Before it can commerce
> With the great universe,
> Takes aim at all the sky
> And starts to ramify.

The implication of this poem is that relationships with the universe and its constituents are indeed possible and even desirable, but that they must occur between "self-defined" entities which are "in time" and have a "shape." Such relationships are the will of "something at the root / More urgent than that urge" to be "vaguely vast"; that is, undifferentiated.[20] Though Wilbur's poems occasionally sound more Emersonian than this one (see, for example, "A Milkweed" from "Two Voices in a Meadow"[21]), Wilbur's Frost-like commitment to particularity is more typical of the orientation that prevails throughout most of his work.

In Wilbur's poetry, the urge deep at the root that prods all things to self-definition and thence to "commerce" with the universe is love. Because the concept of love suffers from imprecision due to overuse in our culture and its literature, Wilbur takes pains to stake out his own conception in poems that clarify what the power of love can and cannot do. Wilbur's sense of the range of possible outcomes when love is at work in the world may be seen in an examination of three poems: "Loves of the Puppets" (*AP:NCP* 187),

---

[20] Wilbur expresses a related thought in "On the Marginal Way": ". . . All things shall be brought, / To the full state and stature of their kind " by a "vast motive" (*WS:NCP* 122). Both poems celebrate the potential of particular persons and things to consort in a spiritual unity which does not require unification.

[21] See Chapter Four, pp. 84-86.

"Cottage Street, 1953" (*MR:NCP* 68), and "Mined Country" (*BC:NCP* 343-4).

"Loves of the Puppets" is one of Wilbur's poems in which personal and cultural sterility stand as formidable obstacles to love.[22] In fact, for most of the poem, love is only a vague hope, having been supplanted by its most prevalent imitations in our culture: sentimentalized romance and lust. Something is already wrong in the first stanza:

> Meeting when all the world was in the bud,
> Drawn each to each by instinct's wooden face,
> These lovers heedful of the mystic blood,
> Fell glassy-eyed into a hot embrace.

Laurentian mysticism is the object of Wilbur's satire here. In the works of D.H. Lawrence, leaving behind one's identity and getting lost in passion (the temptation of Frost's "Putting in the Seed") is often celebrated. Wilbur calls into question Lawrence's enthusiasm by his choice of words and phrases: "puppets," "instinct's wooden face" and "glassy-eyed." He makes it clear that here the lovers' individuality is being diminished rather than surpassed as Lawrence would have it. Furthermore, Lawrence would portray his characters as in step with nature, but there is manifestly an arhythmic relation between Wilbur's lovers and the seasons: "April, unready to be so intense, / Marked time while these outstripped the gentle weather." The poem's middle stanza tells us that love is not realized: the lovers "flew apart the more they came together," and grew "colder as the flesh grew warm." Finally, they lay "exhausted yet unsated," and the question is asked, "Why did their features run with tear on tear, / Until their looks were individuated?" That is, why do these two remain so separate in sexual union? The last two stanzas of the poem are a compact and complex answer to this question:

> One peace implies another, and they cried
> For want of love as if their souls would crack,

---

[22] "She" (*AP:NCP* 193-4) is another notable example.

Till, in despair of being satisfied,
They vowed at least to share each other's lack.

Then maladroitly they embraced once more,
And hollow rang to hollow with a sound
That tuned the brooks more sweetly than before,
And made the birds explode for miles around.

In other words, they experience post-coital peace individually and this "implies" the lonely peace of death and the loneliness of all the "little deaths" they have experienced in failed and disappointed love. At last, however, "in despair" a breakthrough occurs. They embrace honestly; that is, as they are: clumsy, hollow, lacking. One reading of the poem's last two lines understands the sweetly tuned brook and exploding birds to be evidence that true love has been found at last by adding honest self-disclosure to the relationship. There is new-found harmony between lovers and nature: the birds can't contain themselves for all their empathic joy. This reading, however, violates the tone of satiric caricature that has pervaded the poem from the outset, and which, I believe, carries through to the end. The birds may be exploding with song, but more profoundly they represent spring as nature's time for romance and are exploding because the myth they represent has been discredited. So this myth shares the fate of other myths denied in earlier stanzas: the Laurentian myth of "mystic blood" and the cultural myths that lust is love and that love conquers all. Love's victory is real in this poem, but minimal.

"Cottage Street, 1953" (*MR:NCP* 68) is a composite of Wilbur's recollections of Sylvia Plath. Like "Loves of the Puppets," it is a poem that recognizes the strength of the obstacles which the force of love must overcome to bring about unity. However, it contains a more robust affirmation of love's power than "Loves of the Puppets." The poem has stirred controversy, for some critics have taken the view that Wilbur condescends to Plath and lectures her about despair without any real comprehension of her condition. On the other hand, Bruce Michelson argues: "There is nothing snide about the poem. It is meant to recall the powerlessness that Wilbur felt (and must still feel), with his hard-won faith in

the order of things, to speak of that faith to such abject despair."[23]
Michelson's analysis is certainly true to the poem's middle stanzas:

> It is my office to exemplify
> The published poet in his happiness,
> Thus cheering Sylvia, who has wished to die;
> But half-ashamed, and impotent to bless,
>
> I am a stupid life-guard who has found,
> Swept to his shallows by the tide, a girl
> Who, far from shore, has been immensely drowned,
> And stares through water now with eyes of pearl.
>
> How large is her refusal; and how slight
> The genteel chat whereby we recommend
> Life, of a summer afternoon, despite
> The brewing dusk which hints that it may end.

As a poet who tries to resonate with the deepest emotions of others,
Wilbur feels very keenly that it is *his* failure which blocks effective
communication with Sylvia and others like her.   The poem is more
confessional than condescending, for Wilbur takes his place as a person in
need beside those who despair. To that end, the poem depicts both Wilbur
and Plath as recipients of Edna Ward's care. (We are told in a note that Edna
Ward was Wilbur's mother-in-law and a "Wellesley friend" of Sylvia Plath's
mother [*MR:NCP* 111].) Mrs. Ward is the only one at the tea party she has
arranged who is not paralyzed by Sylvia's depression:

> Framed in her phoenix fire-screen, Edna Ward
> Bends to the tray of Canton, pouring tea
> For frightened Mrs. Plath; then, turning toward
> The pale, slumped daughter, and my wife, and me,

---

[23] Bruce Michelson, "Richard Wilbur's *The Mind-Reader*," in Salinger, 133.

> Asks if we would prefer it weak or strong.
> Will we have milk or lemon, she enquires?
> The visit seems already strained and long.
> Each in his turn, we tell her our desires.

Edna Ward ministers with equanimity to the needs of "frightened Mrs. Plath," and confronts the others with a question. On the surface, her question is about tea, but it speaks as well to deeper issues. She "asks if we would prefer it weak or strong. / Will we have milk or lemon, she enquires?" Do those present prefer a vision of life that is weak or strong, with bitterness removed or tartness added? How open are they to receiving love in all its power (which is being offered symbolically)?

In the person of Edna Ward, love triumphs over death. The poem's opening line ("Framed in her phoenix fire-screen") points toward this conclusion. The poem's final stanzas directly reveal that love gives Mrs. Ward the "grace and courage" to approach depression, fear, helplessness, and even death.

> And Edna Ward shall die in fifteen years,
> After her eight-and-eighty summers of
> Such grace and courage as permit no tears,
> The thin hand reaching out, the last word *love,*
>
> Outliving Sylvia who, condemned to live,
> Shall study for a decade, as she must,
> To state at last her brilliant negative
> In poems free and helpless and unjust.

Edna Ward's last word is love, and it endures beyond the "brilliant negative" of Sylvia Plath's words. The younger woman's words are, in the end, "unjust"–that is, disoriented in a world informed by love. It is true that as in "Loves of the Puppets," here, too, love has not conquered all. Wilbur and even Mrs. Ward remain unable to bridge the distance separating them from Miss Plath. They do not save her. Nevertheless, love is a vital force in the life of Edna Ward and in the world Wilbur observes, and in "Cottage Street, 1953" he is able to give testimony to its power.

The power of love to make the many one is celebrated more clearly in "Mined Country" (*BC:NCP* 343-4) than in either "Loves of the Puppets" or "Cottage Street, 1953." Again, stubborn realities stand in love's way, but they are overcome more completely than in the other two poems. "Mined Country" is also a significant work because it carefully differentiates Wilbur's vision of how love brings about unity from the traditional vision of Romanticism:

> They have gone into the gray hills quilled with birches,
> Drag now their cannon up to the chill mountains;
> But it's going to be long before
> Their war's gone for good.

> I tell you it hits at childhood more than churches
> Full up with sky or buried town fountains,
> Rooms laid open or anything
> Cut stone or cut wood,

> Seeing the boys come swinging slow over the grass
> (Like playing pendulum) their silver plates,
> Stepping with care and listening
> Hard for hid metal's cry.

> It's rightly-called-chaste Belphoebe some would miss,
> Some, calendar colts at Kentucky gates;
> But the remotest would guess that
> Some scheme's gone awry.

> Danger is sunk in the pastures, the woods are sly,
> Ingenuity's covered with flowers!
> We thought woods were wise but never
> Implicated, never involved.

Cows in mid-munch go splattered over the sky;
Roses like brush-whores smile from the bowers;
Shepherds must learn a new language; this
Isn't going to be quickly solved.

Sunshiny field grass, the woods floor, are so mixed up
With earliest trusts, you have to pick back
Far past all you have learned, to go
Disinherit the dumb child,

Tell him to trust things alike and never to stop
Emptying things, but not let them lack
Love in some manner restored; to be
Sure the whole world's wild.

"Mined Country" differentiates Wilbur's vision from Romanticism at
two important points. First, Romantic poets think of childhood as a time of
such a clear insight as adults need to try to recapture.[24] In contrast, Wilbur
here suggests that we must "disinherit the . . . child" who is neither prophetic
nor wise but "dumb," naive, in need of tutelage based on experience. Then,
in regard to nature, Wordsworth in "Tintern Abbey" expresses the Romantic
vision of it as the "anchor of my purest thoughts, the nurse, / The guide, the
guardian of my heart, and soul / Of all my moral being." He concludes that
"Nature never did betray / The heart that loved her."[25] In "Mined Country,"
on the other hand, Wilbur reports that his wartime experience revealed that
"Danger is sunk in pastures" and that "woods . . . [may be] sly." The pastoral
version of nature, in other words, which soldiers had incorporated into their
own *Weltanschauungen* by means of "calendar colts" and stories of wood

---

[24]The key text is Wordsworth's "Ode: Intimations of Immortality From
Recollections of Early Childhood," in *Selected Poems and Prefaces*, 186-191.

[25]"Lines: Composed a Few Miles Above Tintern Abbey," lines 109-11, 122-
123.

nymphs, is not tenable in such a world as the soldier knows, where the enemy may arrange for ingenuity to be "covered with flowers." In short, the experience of war has revealed how absurdly inept conventional Romantic cant about the beneficence of nature may be, since the pleasantly bucolic landscape may turn out to be "mined country."

The conclusion of "Mined Country" offers an alternative to the Romantic vision of how humanity and nature are related. But it is not the alternative one might expect–that is, trading in Romanticism's embrace of nature for either the detached objectivity of Realism or the brave engagement of Existentialism. Rather, Wilbur calls for "Love in some manner restored." Just in what manner love is to be restored Wilbur does not say, but the phrase itself and the lines surrounding it hint that Wilbur may have in mind something like a Christian model of reconciliation.[26] Specifically, there is a parallel in the last stanza of "Mined Country" to the paradox of Christian unity. In Christian belief, unity is experienced by those "in Christ" as a proleptic experience of the promised Kingdom. At the same time, Christianity does not deny that Christians continue to exist in a fallen, fragmented world. The comparable paradox in Wilbur's poem juxtaposes "to be / Sure the whole world's wild" with "Love in some manner restored." Thus, reconciliation is *both* "already" and "not yet" in Wilbur's version as it is in Christianity. In an age of great skepticism Wilbur is able to write both honestly and hopefully.[27]

This Christian model for reconciling the One and the Many is one to which Wilbur frequently turns. In "October Maples, Portland" (*AP:NCP* 198), the model is linked to specific scriptural references indicating how thoroughly Wilbur's version has incorporated Christianity's mythos.

---

[26]In Wilbur's "A Christmas Hymn" (*AP:NCP* 225-6), "The worlds are reconciled" by the holy infant's "descent among us."

[27] See Hill, 27, for another interpretation. Hill suggests that "Mined Country" advises a wariness of natural things that can be overcome "once they are seen to be safe." My interpretation is that the poem denies that, short of Kingdom come, things will ever be safe. I believe the poem is saying that Romanticism must be replaced by something like the Christian vision and not merely chastened by the horrors of war.

The leaves, though little time they have to live,
Were never so unfallen as today,
And seem to yield us through a rustled sieve
The very light from which time fell away.

A showered fire we thought forever lost
Redeems the air. Where friends in passing meet,
They parley in the tongues of Pentecost.
Gold ranks of temples flank the dazzled street.

It is a light of maples, and will go;
But not before it washes eye and brain
With such a tincture, such a sanguine glow
As cannot fail to leave a lasting stain.

So Mary's laundered mantle (in the tale
Which, like all pretty tales, may still be true),
Spread on the rosemary-bush, so drenched the pale
Slight blooms in its irradiated hue,

They could not choose but return in blue.

The salient allusion is to Pentecost (stanza two), when (according to the second chapter of *Acts*) God's Holy Spirit entered Jerusalem. It appeared in "tongues as of fire," enabling people who spoke different languages to communicate about "the mighty works of God." In Wilbur's poem, the light of "today" (when a Pentecost-like event occurs) is further invested with holiness by means of a comparison to the light of Eden. Edenic light shone in a time when God's presence was felt directly. Stanza one states that, "The leaves . . . / Were never so *unfallen* as today" (emphasis added), and through them shines "The very light from which time fell away." Eden's light on the Pentecost-like event comes as grace to the speaker surprising him and filling him with wonder: "A showered fire we thought forever lost / Redeems the air." The "friends" who "in passing meet" "parley in the tongues of

Pentecost," discovering a new unity among themselves. The light purifies ("washes eye and brain") and transforms (it "cannot fail to leave a lasting stain.")[28] And, to reinforce his conviction that the experience will be indelible, Wilbur compares it to the legend of the rosemary bush which tells how the blue color of rosemary blossoms came from "Mary's laundered mantle" drying on a bush and drenching "the pale / Slight blooms in its irradiated hue." The concentration of holiness in something of Mary's was so powerful, the legend goes, that the blossoms "could not choose but to return in blue." To end with such a "pretty tale" gives the whole poem "assertorial lightness"[29] and saves it from becoming ponderously emblematic. The tone is further lightened by the fact that in the legend the blossoms turn blue (a color Wilbur associates with the imagination[30]). Though the poem is about spiritual matters, its goal is to invite imaginative participation rather than to command doctrinal assent. In "October Maples, Portland," then, Christian Scripture and tradition provide Wilbur with a conceptual framework and a set of related images which help him describe a moment of wonder which celebrates newly found unity.

Pentecost as a unifying event is also recalled in an earlier poem, "From the Lookout Rock" (*C:NCP* 327-8). But this is a very different poem from "October Maples, Portland." It has a perspective that is reminiscent of Thomas Merton's world-affirming asceticism and represents a significant variation on Wilbur's religiously oriented understanding of how the One and the Many may be reconciled. Douglas Steere summarizes Merton's

---

[28] Thus, light functions in this poem in a way that recalls Christian baptism. For example, in the *Lutheran Book of Worship* (Philadelphia: Board of Publication, Lutheran Church in America, 1978), 124, in the Rite of Holy Baptism, after the minister makes the sign of the cross with oil on the forehead of the baptized, these words are said: "(name), child of God, you have been sealed by the Holy Spirit and marked with the cross of Christ forever."

[29] Philip Wheelwright, *The Burning Fountain: A Study in the Language of Symbolism*, rev. ed. (Bloomington: Indiana University Press, 1968), 92-96.

[30] See also "Digging for China" (*TTW:NCP* 256), "Merlin Enthralled" (*TTW:NCP* 245-6), "Conjuration" (*C:NCP* 282), "Stop" (*AP:NCP* 184), and "For the New Railway Station in Rome" (*TTW:NCP* 277-8).

relationship to the world in the introduction to *Contemplative Prayer*, a volume in which Merton offers spiritual direction to the monastic community.

> From the very outset of this book [Merton] insists that the monk brings into his new life all of the life of the world that he seems to have abandoned and he says frankly that the monk is called to explore the same worldly conflict of sin and aspiration, but to do it more thoroughly and at greater cost than his brothers who are devoted to works of mercy or creativity in the world, and that the monk and the nun "leaves the world only to listen to the deepest voices that he has left behind."[31]

In Merton's work there is a profound affirmation that spiritual unity with all things and persons can be achieved through *ascesis*. Even though the ascetical tone of Wilbur's "From the Lookout Rock" comes from barrenness that is not chosen, it leads to a prayer in the poem's final stanza which resembles Merton's prayers for unity: "Gods of the wind, return again, / . . . And weave the world to harmony."[32]

The moment which inspires this prayer is eschatalogical, with the end of the world coming by means of entropy: "Not with a bang but a whimper," as Eliot put it. In Wilbur's poem, wind, waves, flags, weathervanes, and sailboat rigging come to rest. Noises hush and all is still. In the bay, even sea waves are on the verge of stillness:

> The parching stones along the shore
> Hastily sip the listless waves,
> In doubt the sea will pour them more
> When lull has loitered into calm.

---

[31] Thomas Merton, *Contemplative Prayer* (Garden City, N.Y.: Doubleday and Company, Inc., Image Books, 1971), 11.

[32] This interpretation depends on Wilbur being aware, as surely he must be, that the same Hebrew word is variously translated into English as "spirit," "breath," and "wind." So, when he writes about the wind in "From the Lookout Rock" we may legitimately ask whether an allusion to spirit or breath is being made. In this poem, clearly it is.

As the wind dies down, the breath of life disappears, and the spirit retreats. Then, in the penultimate stanza, a gull dives toward the water, seemingly one more fall toward deathly stillness.

> I from this rock espy a gull
> Riding the raveled last of air
> Who folds his wings, and tips to fall
> Beside the pillar of the sun.
> (The drumhead bay is like a lake,
> A great and waiting skyward stare.)
> The shoreline gives a timbrel shake:
> Our last Icarian moment, done.

As Icarus, the gull connects the natural entropy described in earlier stanzas to failed human aspiration. No heroic effort can reverse nature's trend. But the descending gull is also the Holy Spirit at Pentecost bringing unity and hope for the future. The bay which had been a sign of death ("lull . . . loitered into calm") is in this stanza "A great and waiting skyward stare" receptive to grace. The shoreline's "timbrel shake" is the death-throe of the "last Icarian moment" and also the beginning of nature's revival. The descent of the dove, the moment of grace which comes as nature and human effort fail, leads to prayer:

> Gods of the wind return again,
> For this was not the peace we prayed;
> Intone again your burdened strain,
> And weave the world to harmony,
> Voyage the seed along the breeze,
> Reviving all your former trade,
> Restore the lilting of the trees
> And massive dances of the sea.

All creation waits united in its need. And the need does not go unmet, for in the praying one senses a reversal of the entropic trend: a quickened pace, a renewal of hope based on trust in the "Gods of the wind." Trees, waves, and the human spirit, too, we presume, have another chance to live. The moment of greatest deprivation is the moment of greatest unity and openness to grace.

In the second half of "Lightness" (*BC:NCP* 386-7), the poet's Aunt Virginia is as free from this world as any monk could hope to be: her family and friends find her "in the garden, in her gay shroud / As vague and as self-possessed as a cloud, / Requiring nothing of them anymore." Her self-possession is not to be confused with self-centeredness. She has not drifted away from this world, but has entered its center: ". . . she sat in the heart of her days, / And watched with a look of peculiar praise." She is dying, and yet she brings life to those who visit: "Seeing her . . . / . . . one hand lightly laid on a fatal door, / [They] thought of the health of the sick, and, what mocked their sighing, / Of the strange intactness of the gladly dying."

Like Merton, Aunt Virginia has cultivated an ascetic spirituality which affirms the world through an engagement with the incarnate presence of God. The poem's opening lines prefigure God's entry into the world through Aunt Virginia, alluding to Christ's birth and to Pentecost. The image there is of the wind carrying a bird's nest filled with eggs from its place high in an elm down to the ground. As the nest descends from heaven to earth, it is likened to a "chalice . . . / Of interlaid daintiest timber" which holds new life in the form of "risk-hallowed eggs." Aunt Virginia's husband calls her "Birdie," "his visitor from the valley," for she has come through an encounter with death (like the eggs) and lived to become like the dove in Christian tradition, a manifestation of God's Holy Spirit.

There is literary precedent, too, for Wilbur's world-affirming asceticism. He himself wrote an extremely insightful essay on Emily Dickinson entitled "Sumptuous Destitution" (*R* 3-15). Wilbur reports that "three major privations" created a gulf between Dickinson and those things she wanted most. "She was deprived of an orthodox and steady religious faith; she was deprived of love; she was deprived of literary recognition" (*R* 5). One of the ways she dealt with "her sentiment of lack" was to assert "the paradox that privation is more plentiful than plenty" (*R* 7). Wilbur posits, for example, that in her poem which begins, "Success is counted sweetest / By those who ne'er succeed," "Emily Dickinson is arguing the *superiority* of defeat to victory, of frustration to satisfaction, and of anguished comprehension to mere possession. . . . The victors . . . have paid for their triumph by a sacrifice of awareness. . . . For the dying soldier, the case is reversed: . . . material loss has led to spiritual gain" (*R* 9-10). Furthermore, Dickinson differentiates between appetite, which can only be satisfied by possession of the "object in itself," and desire in which the "object is spiritually possessed, not merely for itself, but more truly as an index of the All. . . . Emily Dickinson elected the economy of desire, and . . . came to live in a huge world of delectable distances" (*R* 11).

One of Wilbur's poems which clearly echoes Dickinson's argument for the "superiority of defeat to victory" is "A Voice From Under the Table" (*TTW:NCP* 247-8). The voice belongs to one who has drunk himself into "this low distress." While in the horizontal position from which he is unable to move, he holds forth in drunken soliloquy, commenting upon wine, women, nature, literature, and most of all, love. He has not possessed the objects of his desire, but he savors them from a distance. He disagrees with the "devil" who "told me it was all the same / Whether to fail by spirit or by sense," for it is his objective failures which have allowed his robust spirit to gain so much. "The end of thirst exceeds experience," he concludes, and so he is proud to be "a sort of martyr, as you see, / A horizontal monument to patience," offering himself willingly to drunkenness and its "delectable distances" (*R* 11) from the world:

> The calves of waitresses parade about
> My helpless head upon this sodden floor.
> Well, I am down again, but not yet out.
> O sweet frustrations, I shall be back for more.

Some readers of "A Voice . . ." might think Wilbur is mocking Dickinson. But because Wilbur takes the same philosophical stance toward "sumptuous destitution" in other poems, as well as in his essay on Dickinson, the speaker of "A Voice From Under the Table" ought to be seen as reliable—in spite of his drunkenness, his occasional belligerence and cynicism and silliness ("I toast the birds in the burning trees"). In spite of everything, this voice is one that celebrates.

"Grasse: The Olive Trees" (*C:NCP* 304-5) does not directly affirm asceticism, but it denies that sensuality alone can satisfy the longings of the human spirit. In "Ballade for the Duke of Orléans" (*AP:NCP* 211-12) and in "The Giaour and Pacha," (*BC:NCP* 352) destitution is portrayed as sumptuous primarily because pursuit is preferable to possession. In these three poems and in more than a dozen others scattered throughout Wilbur's work, the unity that is made possible by means of imaginative possession is celebrated over that which is possible through physical possession. The dilemma of the One and the Many is resolved spiritually and emotionally in the paradoxical truth of "sumptuous destitution."

Like others in his generation, Richard Wilbur has worked toward renewing poetry and making it more celebrative by being attentive to non-rational forces that affect our lives. Unlike many of his peers who in the fifties and sixties tried to substitute the non-rational for the rational in poetry, he has tried to elevate the non-rational without dispensing with the rational. To that end, he has probed for signs of a suprarational spirit in a world that often appears to be void of beauty and threatened by chaos. By means of elegant formal poetry, Wilbur reveals *how* he has come to his spiritual and theological insights and *what* they are. He has adopted the traditional structures of meditative poetry and perceived the "invisible in the visible" as his observation of the world deepens to contemplation. He comes to the same end by tracking the transformation of dialectically related phenomena and by taking on the perspectives of liminality. Those willing to suspend their disbelief and enter Wilbur's poetry will find themselves carried along as Wilbur moves again and again toward spiritually significant insights. Wilbur's poems lead us to abandon the mindsets we use day-to-day and to "stand outside" our normal selves in *ecstasis.*

Wilbur's ecstatic vision is not of "distinction . . . destroyed, but [of] separateness . . . overcome."[33] Unlike Emersonian idealism which strives toward unity with the essence of all things in a purely spiritual state, Wilbur's vision sees spirit and matter as inextricably intertwined. Like Robert Frost, Wilbur embraces an earthly spirituality, and finds abstractions to be

---

[33] Allchin, 57.

spiritually as well as physically empty. Among traditional Christian teachings, therefore, the incarnation and the story of Pentecost find deep resonance in Wilbur's verse. He often alludes to them, treating them as prototypical for the way love and grace unite spirit and matter. Deep involvement in the tangible world is thus portrayed as spiritually significant in Wilbur's poems, though he also celebrates the possibility that one may be spiritually at one with the things of this world without being in close physical proximity to them.

This is the unifying thread throughout Wilbur's work and his profound contribution to American literature in the latter half of our century: he has had an abiding fascination with the potential of formal verse for expressing "the relation of the One with the Many, the leap by which infinity becomes finite, essence becomes existence; the commingling of the spirit with matter, the working of God in the world."[34]

---

[34] Nemerov, in Salinger, 43.

WORKS CONSULTED

I. Primary Sources

A. Wilbur
Wilbur, Richard. *The Beautiful Changes and Other Poems.* New York: Reynal and Hitchcock, 1947.
—. *Ceremony and Other Poems.* New York: Harcourt, Brace and Co., 1950.
—. "The Genie in the Bottle." In *Mid-Century American Poets*, edited by John Ciardi, 1-17. New York: Twayne Publishers, Inc., 1950.
—. *The Poet Speaks.* WGBH Radio Broadcast. Boston, Massachusetts. Feb. 11, 1952. 2 Tapes. Lamont Library, Harvard University.
—. "A Game of Catch." *New Yorker* 29 (July 18, 1953): 74-76.
—, comp. *A Bestiary.* Illustrations by Alexander Calder. New York: Pantheon Books, 1955.
—. "Poetry and The Landscape." In *The New Landscape in Art and Science*, edited by Gyorgy Kepes. Chicago: Theobald, 1956.
—. *Things of This World, Poems by Richard Wilbur.* New York: Harcourt, Brace and Co., 1956.
Candide, A Comic Operetta Based on Voltaire's Satire. Lyrics by Richard Wilbur, Book by Lillian Hellman, Score by Leonard Bernstein, Other Lyrics by John Latouche and Dorothy Parker. Toronto: Random House, 1957.
—. *Poems 1943-1956.* London: Faber and Faber, 1957.
—, intro. and ed. *Poe: Complete Poems.* By Edgar Allen Poe. New York: Dell Books, 1959.
—. *The Poems of Richard Wilbur: Read by the Author.* Spoken Arts 747. 1959. 1 disc. 26 poems.
—. *Advice to a Prophet and Other Poems.* New York: Harcourt, Brace and World, Inc., 1961.
—. "A Poem of Dedication for Lincoln Center." *New York Times* 112 (September 24, 1962): 34.
—. *Richard Wilbur Reading Selections from His Poetry.* Morris Gray Lecture. Harvard University. Nov. 21, 1963. Boston: Fassett Recording Studio. 2 discs. Lamont Library, Harvard University.—. *Richard Wilbur Reading His Own*

Poems and Translations. Boston. Transradio Recording. 1 disc. Lamont Library, Harvard University.

—. Comment on three critiques of "Love Calls Us to the Things of This World." In *The Contemporary Poet as Artist and Critic: Eight Symposia*, edited by Anthony Ostroff, 17-21. Boston: Little, Brown, 1964.

—, trans. *The Misanthrope and Tartuffe.* By Jean Baptiste Poquelin de Molière. New York: Harcourt Brace and World, Inc., A Harvest Book, 1965.

—. Letter to George Abbot White, 31 December 1967.

—. *Walking to Sleep: New Poems and Translations.* New York: Harcourt Brace Jovanovich, 1969.

—, trans. *The School for Wives.* By Jean Baptiste Poquelin de Molière. New York: Harcourt Brace Jovanovich, 1971.

—. *Opposites.* New York: Harcourt Brace Jovanovich, 1973.

—. *The Mind-Reader: New Poems by Richard Wilbur.* New York: Harcourt Brace Jovanovich, 1976.

—. *Responses: Prose Pieces, 1953-1976.* New York: Harcourt Brace Jovanovich, 1976.

—. "The Art of Poetry." An interview by P. Still, E.C. High, and E.M. Elllison. *Paris Review* 19 (Winter 1977): 69-105.

—, trans. "Mr. T.S. Eliot Cooking Pasta." By Jozsef Tornai. *New Yorker* 53:2 (February 28, 1977): 35.

—. "The Poetry of Witter Bynner." *American Poetry Review* 6 (November-December 1977): 3-8.

—, trans. *The Learned Ladies.* By Jean Baptiste Poquelin de Molière. New York: Harcourt Brace Jovanovich, 1978.

—. "Shad Time." *New Yorker* 54:15 (May 29, 1978): 30.

—, trans. "Six Years Later." By Joseph Brodsky. *New Yorker* 54:46 (January 1, 1979): 30.

—. "Transit." *New Yorker* 54:48 (January 15, 1979): 38.

—. "Icarium Mare." *New Yorker* 55:18 (June 18, 1979): 34.

—. "For W.H. Auden." *Atlantic* 244:4 (October 1979): 98.

—. "Elizabeth Bishop." *Ploughshares* 6:2 (1980): 10-14.

—, trans. "Mirabeau Bridge." By Guillaume Apollinaire. *Paris Review* 23:81 (Autumn, 1981): 110.

—. "Some Differences." *Massachusetts Review* 22:4 (Winter, 1981): 778-9.

—, trans. *Andromache: Tragedy in Five Acts, 1667.* By Jean Racine. New York: Harcourt Brace Jovanovich, 1982.

—. "Poe and the Art of Suggestion." *University of Mississippi: Studies in English* 3 (1982): 1-13.

—. *The Whale and Other Uncollected Translations.* Brockport, New York: Boa Editions, Ltd., 1982.

—. "Hamlen Brook." *Poetry* 141:1 (October 1982): 25.

—. "Lying." *New Yorker* 58 (January 24, 1983): 36.

—. "A Finished Man." *New Yorker* 61 (March 4, 1985): 42.

---. "A Word from Cummington." In *Under Open Sky: Poets on William Cullen Bryant.* Ed. Norbert Krapf. New York: Fordham University Press, 1986. 29-32.

---. *New and Collected Poems.* San Diego: Harcourt Brace Jovanovich, 1988.

---. "Ash Wednesday." *Yale Review* 78:2 (Winter 1989): 215-17.

---. "The Persistence of Riddles." *Yale Review* 78:3 (Spring 1989): 333-51.

---. *Conversations with Richard Wilbur.* Edited by William Butts. Jackson: University Press of Mississippi, 1990.

---. *More Opposites: Poems and Drawings by Richard Wilbur.* New York: Harcourt Brace Jovanovich, 1991.

B. Primary Sources Other Than Wilbur

Allen, Donald, ed. *The New American Poetry.* New York: Grove Press, Inc., 1960.

Allen, Gay Wilson, Walter B. Rideout, and James K. Robinson. *American Poetry.* New York: Harper and Row, 1965.

Ashberry, John. *A Wave: Poems.* New York: Viking Penguin Books, 1984.

Carroll, Lewis. *Alice's Adventures in Wonderland.* New York: Random House, 1946.

---. *Through the Looking Glass: And What Alice Found There.* New York: Random House, 1946.

Coleridge, Samuel Taylor. *Biographia Literaria.* Edited by George Watson. London: J.M. Dent and Sons, 1956.

---. *Selected Poetry and Prose of Coleridge.* Edited by Donald A. Stauffer. New York: Random House, The Modern Library, 1951.

Dickinson, Emily. *Final Harvest: Emily Dickinson's Poems.* Selection and Introduction by Thomas H. Johnson. Boston: Little, Brown and Company, 1961.

Eliot, T.S. *The Complete Poems and Plays: 1909-1950.* New York: Harcourt, Brace & World, Inc., 1971.

Ellman, Richard, and Robert O'Clair, eds. *The Norton Anthology of Modern Poetry.* New York: W.W. Norton and Co., Inc., 1973.

Emerson, Ralph Waldo. *Selections from Ralph Waldo Emerson.* Edited by Stephen E. Whicher. Boston: Houghton Mifflin Company, 1957.

Frost, Robert. *The Poetry of Robert Frost.* Edited by Edward Connery Lathem. New York: Holt, Rinehart and Winston, 1969.

Gardner, Helen, ed. *The Metaphysical Poets.* Baltimore: Penguin Books, 1957.

O'Hara, Frank. *The Selected Poems of Frank O'Hara.* Edited by Donald Allen. New York: Vintage Books, A Division of Random House, 1974.

Stevens, Wallace. *The Collected Poems of Wallace Stevens.* New York: Alfred A. Knopf, 1978.

Warren, Robert Penn. *New and Selected Poems 1923-1985.* New York: Random House, 1985.

Whitman, Walt. *Leaves of Grass.* Edited by Sculley Bradley and Harold W. Blodgett. New York: W.W. Norton & Company, Inc., 1973.

Wordsworth, William. *Selected Poems and Prefaces by William Wordworth.* Edited by Jack Stillinger. Boston: Houghton Mifflin Company, 1965.

Zaranka, William, ed. *The Brand-X Anthology of Poetry.* Cambridge: Apple-wood Books, Inc., 1981.

II. Secondary Sources

A. Criticism

Altieri, Charles. *Enlarging the Temple: New Directions in American Poetry during the 1960s.* London: Associated University Presses, Inc., 1979.

Bedient, Calvin. Review of *The Mind Reader*, by Richard Wilbur. *The New Republic* 174 (June 5, 1976): 21-22.

Breslin, James E.B. *From Modern to Contemporary: American Poetry 1945-1965.* Chicago: The University of Chicago Press, 1984.

Brooker, Jewel Spears. "A Conversation With Richard Wilbur." *Christianity and Literature* 42, no. 4 (Summer 1993): 517-539.

Brooks, Cleanth. "This World and More: "The Poetry of Richard Wilbur." *Christianity and Literature* 42, no. 4 (Summer 1993): 541-550.

Cummins, Paul F. *Richard Wilbur: A Critical Essay.* Contemporary Writers in Christian Perspective. Ed. Roderick Jellema; Grand Rapids: William B. Eerdmans, 1971.

Dickey, James. *Babel to Byzantium: Poets and Poetry Now.* New York: Farrar, Strauss & Giroux, 1968.

Dinneen, Marcia B. "Richard Wilbur: A Bibliography of Secondary Sources." *Bulletin of Bibliography* 37, no. 1 (Jan.-Mar. 1980): 16-22.

Drake, Leah Bodine. "New Voices in Poetry." *The Atlantic,* 199 (June, 1957): 75-78.

Faas, Ekbert. *Towards a New American Poetics: Essays and Interviews.* Santa Barbara: Black Sparrow Press, 1979.

Field, John P. *Richard Wilbur: A Bibliographical Checklist.* The Kent State University Press, 1971.

Gross, Harvey. *Sound and Form in Modern Poetry: A Study of Prosody from Thomas Hardy to Robert Lowell.* Ann Arbor: The University of Michigan Press, 1968.

Hall, Donald. "Method in Poetic Composition: With Special Attention to Richard Eberhart and Richard Wilbur." *Paris Review* no. 3 (Autumn, 1953): 113-119.

Hamilton, Ian. "A Talent of the Shallows." *Times Literary Supplement,* 15-21 (September 1989): 999-1000.

Harrigan, Anthony. "American Formalists." *The South Atlantic Quarterly* 49 (October, 1950): 483-89.

Harris, Peter. "Forty Years of Richard Wilbur: The Loving Work of an Equilibrist." *Virginia Quarterly Review* 66 (Summer 1990) : 412-25.

Hill, Donald L. *Richard Wilbur.* New York: Twayne Publishers, Inc., 1967.

Jarrell, Randall. *Poetry and the Age.* New York: Vintage Books, 1953.

Johnson, Kenneth. "Virtues in Style, Defect in Content: The Poetry of Richard Wilbur." In *The Fifties: Fiction, Poetry, Drama,* edited by Warren French, 209-16. Deland, Florida: Everett/Edwards Inc., 1970.

Kunitz, Stanley, ed. *Twentieth Century Authors*, First Supplement, 1079-1080. New York: The R.W. Wilson Co., 1955.

Leithauser, Brad. "America's Master of Formal Verse." *New Republic* 186 (March 24, 1982): 28-31.

Lingeman, R.R. "Sunday Poets." *New York Times Book Review* 83 (August, 1978): 35.

Michelson, Bruce. "Richard Wilbur's Music of Pure Gold." *Christianity and Literature* 42, no. 4 (Summer 1993): 585-600.

---. *Wilbur's Poetry: Music in a Scattering Time.* Amherst: The University of Massachusetts Press, 1991.

Ostroff, Anthony, ed. *The Contemporary Poet as Artist and Critic: Eight Symposia.* Boston: Little, Brown and Co., 1964.

Park, Clara Claiborne. "Called to Praise: Richard Wilbur's Brilliant Positive." *Christianity and Literature* 42, no. 4 (Summer 1993): 551-567.

Payne, Marjory Scheidt. "Doubt and Redeeming Gaiety: Religious and Philosophical Strands in Richard Wilbur's Poetry." *Christianity and Literature* 42, no. 4 (Summer 1993): 569-583.

Reedy, Gerard. "The Senses of Richard Wilbur." *Renascence* 21 (Spring, 1969): 145-50.

Salinger, Wendy, ed. *Richard Wilbur's Creation.* Ann Arbor: The University of Michigan Press, 1983.

Scott, Nathan A. "Literalist of the Imagination." *Christian Century* 75 (March 19, 1958): 344.

---. "The Poetry of Richard Wilbur - 'The Spendour of Mere Being.'" *Christianity and Literature* 39:1 (Autumn 1989):7-33.

Stitt, Peter. *The World's Hieroglyphic Beauty: Five American Poets.* Athens: The University of Georgia Press, 1985.

Vendler, Helen. *Part of Nature, Part of Us: Modern American Poets.* Cambridge: Harvard University Press, 1980.

Weatherhead, A.K. "Richard Wilbur: Poetry of Things." *ELH* 35 (December, 1968): 606-17.

B. Literature and Art: History and Theory

Abrams, M.H. *A Glossary of Literary Terms*, 3rd ed. New York: Holt, Rinehart and Winston, Inc., 1971.

---. *Natural Supernaturalism: Tradition and Revolution in Romantic Literature.* New York: W.W. Norton and Co., 1971.

Adams, Hazard, ed. *Critical Theory Since Plato.* New York: Harcourt Brace Jovanovich, Inc., 1971.

Allen, Donald, and Warren Tallman, eds. *The Poetics of the New American Poetry.* New York: Grove Press, Inc., 1973.

Altieri, Charles. "From Symbolist Thought to Immanence: The Ground of Postmodern American Poetry." *Boundary* 2 1, 3 (Spring, 1973): 605-42.

Brooks, Cleanth. *The Well Wrought Urn: Studies in the Structure of Poetry.* New York: Harcourt, Brace & World, Inc., 1947.

128   *Ecstasy Within Discipline*

---, and Robert Penn Warren. *Understanding Poetry*, 4th ed. New York: Holt, Rinehart and Winston, 1976.

Ciardi, John. *How Does A Poem Mean?* Boston: Houghton Mifflin Company, 1959.

Fuchs, Eric. "The Mutual Questioning of Ethics and Aesthetics." *Cross Currents* 43:1 (Spring, 1993): 26-37.

Fussell, Paul. *Poetic Meter and Poetic Form*, rev. ed. New York: Random House, 1979.

Graff, Gerald. *Literature Against Itself: Literary Ideas in Modern Society.* Chicago: University of Chicago Press, 1979.

Gross, Harvey, ed. *The Structure of Verse: Modern Essays on Prosody*, rev. ed. New York: The Ecco Press, 1979.

Gunn, Giles. *The Interpretation of Otherness: Literature, Religion and The American Imagination.* New York: Oxford University Press, 1979.

Hoffman, Daniel. "Poetry: After Modernism." In *Harvard Guide to Contemporary American Writing*, edited by Daniel Hoffman, 439-95. Cambridge: The Belknap Press of Harvard University Press, 1979.

---. "Poetry: Dissidents From Schools." In *Harvard Guide to Contemporary American Writing*, edited by Daniel Hoffman, 564-606. Cambridge: The Belknap Press of Harvard University Press, 1979.

---. "Poetry: Schools of Dissidents." In *Harvard Guide to Contemporary American Writing*, edited by Daniel Hoffman, 496-593. Cambridge: The Belknap Press of Harvard University Press, 1979.

Holman, C. Hugh. *A Handbook to Literature: Based on the Original by William Flint Thrall and Addison Hibbard*, 3rd ed. Indianapolis: The Bobbs-Merrill Company, Inc., 1972.

Holquist, Michael. *Dialogism: Bakhtin and his World.* London: Routledge, 1990.

Iser, Wolfgang. *The Art of Reading: A Theory of Aesthetic Response.* Baltimore: The Johns Hopkins University Press, 1978.

Jones, Howard Mumford. *Belief and Disbelief in American Literature.* Chicago: University of Chicago Press, 1967.

Kort, Wesley A. *Narrative Elements and Religious Meaning.* Philadelphia: Fortress Press, 1975.

Langbaum, Robert. "The New Nature Poetry." In his *The Modern Spirit: Essays on the Continuity of Nineteenth and Twentieth Century Literature.* London: Chatto and Windus, 1970.

---. *The Poetry of Experience: The Dramatic Monologue in Modern Literary Tradition.* New York: W.W. Norton and Company, Inc., 1957.

Levertov, Denise. *The Poet in the World.* New York: A New Directions Book, 1973.

Lewis, R.W.B. *The American Adam: Innocence, Tragedy, and Tradition in the Nineteenth Century.* Chicago: The University of Chicago Press, 1955.

Martz, Louis L. *The Poem of the Mind: Essays on Poetry/English and American.* London: Oxford University Press, 1966.

---. *The Poetry of Meditation: A Study in English Religious Literature of the Seventeenth Century*, rev. ed. New Haven: Yale University Press, 1962.

---. *The Wit of Love: Donne, Carew, Crashaw, Marvell.* Notre Dame, Indiana: The University of Notre Dame Press, 1969.

McShine, Kynaston, ed. *The Natural Paradise: Painting in America 1800-1950.* New York: The Museum of Modern Art, 1976.

Menzel, Daniel A. *A Field Guide to the Stars and Planets.* Boston: Houghton Mifflin Company, 1964.

Milosz, Czeslaw. *The Witness of Poetry: The Charles Eliot Norton Lectures 1981-82.* Cambridge: Harvard University Press, 1983.

Nemerov, Howard. *Figures of Thought: Speculations on the Meaning of Poetry and Other Essays.* Boston: David R. Godine, Publisher, Inc., 1978.

Petersson, Robert T. *The Art of Ecstasy: Teresa, Bernini, and Crashaw.* London: Routledge and Kegan Paul, 1970.

Praz, Mario. *Mnemosyne: The Parallel Between Literature and the Visual Arts.* Princeton: Princeton University Press, 1970.

Scott, Nathan A., Jr. "The Poetry and Theology of Earth: Reflections on the Testimony of Joseph Sittler and Gerard Manley Hopkins." *The Journal of Religion* 54, no. 2 (April, 1974): 102-18.

---. *The Wild Prayer of Longing: Poetry and the Sacred.* New Haven: Yale University Press, 1971.

Tanner, Tony. *The Reign of Wonder: Naivety and Reality in American Literature.* New York: Harper and Row, 1967.

Turco, Lewis. *The Book of Forms: A Handbook of Poetics.* New York: E.P. Dutton and Co., Inc., 1968.

Waggoner, Hyatt H. *American Visionary Poetry.* Baton Rouge: L.S.U. Press, 1982.

---. *American Poets: From the Puritans to the Present.* Boston: Houghton Mifflin Co., 1968.

Welleck, Rene. *The Attack on Literature and Other Essays.* Chapel Hill: The University of North Carolina Press, 1982.

Wheelwright, Philip. *The Burning Fountain: A Study in the Language of Symbolism,* rev. ed. Bloomington, Indiana: Indiana University Press, 1968.

Wimsatt, William K., Jr., and Cleanth Brooks. *Literary Criticism: A Short History.* 2 vols. Chicago: The University of Chicago Press, 1957.

C. Theology and Philosophy

Allchin, A.M. *The World is a Wedding: Explorations in Christian Spirituality.* New York: Crossroad Publishing Company, 1982.

Beardsley, Monroe C. *Aesthetics: From Classical Greece to the Present.* University, Alabama: The University of Alabama Press, 1966.

Black, John. *The Dominion of Man: The Search for Ecological Responsibility.* Edinburgh: The University Press, 1970.

Bonifazi, Conrad. *A Theology of Things.* Philadelphia: J.B. Lippincott Co., 1967.

Brown, Frank Burch. *Religious Aesthetics: A Theological Study of Making and Meaning.* Princeton: Princeton University Press, 1989.

Clissold, Stephen. *St. Teresa of Avila.* London: Sheldon Press, 1979.

Cobb, John B., Jr. *God and World*. Philadelphia: The Westminster Press, 1969.

Cousins, Kathryn and Cousins, Ewert, with Richard J. Payne. *How to Read a Spiritual Book*. New York: Paulist Press, 1981.

Cox, Harvey. *The Secular City*. New York: The Macmillan Company, 1965.

Derrick, Christopher. *The Delicate Creation: Towards a Theology of the Environment*. Old Greenwich, Connecticut: The Devin-Adair Co., 1971.

Ebeling, Gerhard. *God and Word*. Trans. James W. Leitch. Philadelphia: Fortress Press, 1967.

---. *Luther: An Introduction to His Thought*. Trans. R.A. Wilson. Philadelphia: Fortress Press, 1972.

Egan, Harvey D.S.J. *What Are They Saying About Mysticism?* New York: Paulist Press, 1982.

Elder, Frederick. *Crisis in Eden: A Religious Study of Man and Environment*. Nashville: Abingdon Press, 1970.

Eliada, Mircea. *Myth and Reality*. Trans. Willard R. Trask. New York: Harper and Row, 1963.

Fleming, David L., S.J. *The Spiritual Exercises of St. Ignatius: A Literal Translation and A Contemporary Reading*. St. Louis: The Institute of Jesuit Sources, 1978.

Franck, Frederick. *The Zen of Seeing: Seeing/Drawing as Meditation*. New York: Random House, 1973.

Frazer, Sir James. *The New Golden Bough: A New Abridgement of the Classic Work by Sir James George Frazer*. Edited by Theodor H. Gaster. New York: The New American Library, Inc., Mentor Books, 1964.

Gerrish, Brian A. *Grace and Reason: A Study in the Theology of Luther*. Chicago: The University of Chicago Press, Midway reprint, 1979.

Harned, David Baily. *Grace and the Common Life*. Charlottesville: The University Press of Virginia, 1971.

Hefner, Philip J., ed. *The Scope of Grace: Essays on Nature and Grace in Honor of Joseph Sittler*. Philadelphia: Fortress Press, 1964.

Huizinga, John. *Homo Ludens: A Study of the Play Element in Culture*. Boston: Beacon Press, 1955.

Inter-Lutheran Commission on Worship. *Lutheran Book of Worship*. Philadelphia: Board of Publication, Lutheran Church in America, 1978.

Keen, Sam. *Apology for Wonder*. New York: Harper and Row, 1969.

Logan, James C. "The Secularization of Nature." In *Christians and the Good Earth*. Addresses and Discussions at the Third National Conference of the Faith-Man-Nature Group. 24-25 Nov. 1967. Alexandria, Virginia: The Faith-Man-Nature Group.

McFague, Sallie. *Models for God: Theology for an Ecological, Nuclear Age*. Philadelphia: Fortress Press, 1987.

Merton, Thomas. *Contemplative Prayer*. Garden City, N.Y.: Doubleday and Co., Inc., 1971.

Meyendorff, John. *St. Gregory Palamas and Orthodox Spirituality*. Trans. Adele Fiske. n.p. St. Vladimir's Seminary Press, 1974.

Moltmann, Jürgen. "Three Lectures on the Theology of Hope." *Kalamazoo College Review* 32, no. 3 (1970): 3-24.

Niebuhr, H. Richard. *Christ and Culture*. New York: Harper and Brothers, 1951.

---. *The Meaning of Revelation*. New York: The Macmillan Company, 1941.

Nouwen, Henri J.M. *The Genesee Diary: Report from a Trappist Monastery*. Garden City, N.Y.: Doubleday and Co., Inc., 1976.

---. *The Way of the Heart: Desert Spirituality and Contemporary Writings*. New York: The Seabury Press, 1981.

Otto, Rudolph. *The Idea of the Holy*, second ed. Trans. John W. Harvey. London: Oxford University Press, 1950.

Owens, Virginia Stem. *And The Trees Claps Their Hands: Faith, Perception, and the New Physics*. Grand Rapids: William B. Eerdmans Publishing Co., 1983.

Palmer, Parker. *To Know As We Are Known: A Spirituality of Education*. San Francisco: Harper and Row, 1983.

Prenter, Regin. *Spiritus Creator*. Trans. John M. Jensen. Philadelphia: Muhlenberg Press, 1953.

Santmire, H. Paul. *Brother Earth: Nature, God and Ecology in Time of Crisis*. New York: Thomas Nelson, Inc., 1970.

Schmemann, Alexander. *For the Life of the World: Sacraments and Orthodoxy*. n.p. St. Vladimir's Seminary Press, 1973.

Sittler, Joseph. "Called to Unity." *The Eucmenical Review* 14, no. 2 (January, 1962): 177-87.

---. *Essays on Nature and Grace*. Philadelphia: Fortress Press, 1972.

Tappert, Theodore G. Trans. and ed. *The Book of Concord*. Philadelphia: Fortress Press, 1969.

Turner, Victor. *Dramas, Fields, and Metaphors: Symbolic Action in Human Society*. Ithaca: Cornell University Press, 1974.

Vagaggini, Cipriano, O.S.B. *The Flesh, Instrument of Salvation: A Theology of the Human Body*. New York: Alba House, 1969.

Watson, Philip S. *Let God Be God: An Interpretation of the Theology of Martin Luther*. Philadelphia: Fortress Press, 1947.

White, Lynn, Jr. "The Historical Roots of Our Ecological Crisis." *Science* 155 (March 10, 1967): 1203-7.

Wilder, Amos N. *The New Voice: Religion, Literature, Hermeneutics*. New York: Herder and Herder, 1969.

---. *Theopoetic: Theology and the Religious Imagination*. Philadelphia: Fortress Press, 1976.